Anonymous

Notes of hospital life

From November, 1861 to August, 1863

Anonymous

Notes of hospital life
From November, 1861 to August, 1863

ISBN/EAN: 9783337235277

Printed in Europe, USA, Canada, Australia, Japan

Cover: Foto ©Andreas Hilbeck / pixelio.de

More available books at **www.hansebooks.com**

NOTES

of

HOSPITAL LIFE

FROM NOVEMBER, 1861, TO AUGUST, 1863.

"Je viens de faire un ouvrage."
"Comment! un livre?"
"Non; pas un livre; je ne suis pas si bête!"

PHILADELPHIA:

J. B. LIPPINCOTT & CO.

1864.

CONTENTS.

TO

THE PRIVATES

Army of the United States;

WHOSE

DARING IN DANGER;
PATIENCE IN PRIVATION;
SELF-SACRIFICE IN SUFFERING;
AND LOYALTY IN LOVE FOR THEIR COUNTRY,

HAVE GIVEN TO THE WORLD A NOBLE EXAMPLE,
WORTHY OF ALL IMITATION,

These Notes are affectionately Dedicated,

BY ONE WHOSE PRIVILEGE IT IS TO
HAVE BEEN PERMITTED
TO MINISTER TO THE SICK AND WOUNDED AMONG THEM,
IN ONE OF OUR

CITY HOSPITALS.

INTRODUCTION.

THESE " Notes " need no introduction. They were jotted down, from day to day, as a private journal, and are printed only at the instance of friends. The undersigned greatly mistakes if they are not welcomed as an accession to our literature. On every page they betray a large and elegant culture, and what is better, they manifest a profound sympathy in all that is human, and a keen insight into nature and into man's heart. Felicities of thought and expression abound, vivid pictures of incidents and life-like sketches of character. They are full of spirit, of wisdom, and of right feeling.

They rise, too, to the level of a great subject. In the conflict which convulses our land, how many souls are stirred — how many hearts made to burn! We cannot envy him or her who can look on such a scene—on the principles involved, and the interests at stake, and yet not feel kindled to a higher life. We can regard but with compassion those who see in this war only blunders to be criticised, absurdities to be ridiculed, crimes to be gloated over, or life and property to be deplored.

If, in the liberty and peace of those who live in this land, and of the millions who are to come after, there be anything precious; if there is anything sacred and venerable in the unity of a great people and in the sovereignty with which they have been charged by solemn compact; if there is any claim upon us as men and as Christians, in behalf of a race that has suffered long and sorely at our hands, and that now, for the first time, seems to behold the light of hope, then is there that at stake which should move every one to sympathy and to help.

Our hearts must bleed as we gaze on the vast suffering; but "we buy our blessings at a price." Hitherto it has been our great danger that we have had little save sunshine. Prosperity, great and uninterrupted, is perilous for nations as well as individuals. It is amidst thunder-clouds, and storms, that the oak gets strength and deep root; it is while battling in tempestuous seas that the vessel proves and at the same time confirms her capacity. So in this gigantic strife, powers will be elicited, and a trust in God and in grand principles developed, which will be, we trust, our fortress and our high tower hereafter.

It is one of the merits of this writer that, with a heart alive to the wants and wretchedness of the sick and wounded, she joins discernment of the mighty questions involved. She sees, with exquisite relish, the picturesque in character and incident; she has an eye, too, for the deep wealth of affection and generous sympathy that lie embedded in the roughest natures — for the flashes of merriment and drollery which lighten up the darkest scenes—for the delicate tastes and noble sentiments that often possess those whose hands have been hardened by toil, and whose minds (in the judgment of too many) must needs have been debased by habitual contact with vulgar pursuits. Hers is a heart which can feel that which makes all the world akin—which can see that labor does not degrade, but rather elevates those who pursue it in the true spirit; and that nothing can be more preposterous in a land like ours, which is made and glorified by the joint handiwork of God and

man, than to decry or despise it. These pages
are instinct with faith in God and in our people;
with hope for the future; with a charity that
never faileth.

A. POTTER.

PHILADELPHIA, February, 1864.

PREFACE.

A LITERARY friend said to me some time since, "One of the greatest evils of this rebellion, is the manner in which it is tainting our literature, science, and arts. If they would only fight it out and confine it to fighting, bad as it is, we might rise from its effects; but this flood of war-literature will so set the mind of the next genera-tion into a military groove, that poetry, refined taste, and love for the beautiful, will be lost in the roar of literary drums and mental musketry."

"And did you imagine," said I, "that such a rebellion could be carried on without affecting and injuring every nerve and fibre of the whole country? Do you not see that it is a moral Pyæmia — a poisoning of the veins of the entire nation? And although we trust the disease may be arrested ere it destroy national existence, still the system suffers throughout; and the result must

be vapid volumes, paltry pictures, and silly statements of so-called science. But granting that it
is to be deplored—that the military mind should
take the place of the literary one, I must break
a lance with you on the question whether, in so
doing, 'poetry, refined taste, and love for the
beautiful' must of necessity be lost. I will not
grant it. At the opening of the war I thought,
with you, that the finer feelings of our nature were
exclusively the property of the higher classes; but
two years' experience in a military hospital, where
men appear mentally as well as physically in "undress uniform," has shown me the utter fallacy of
such a theory; and now I do not hesitate to affirm
that I have seen there as much unwritten poetry,
tender feeling, aye, and love for the beautiful, as I
have ever witnessed among the same number of
people gathered together at any time, or in any
place."

Sickly sentimentality, whether shown in words
or actions, for "our poor, suffering soldiers," is certainly a thing to be much deprecated; but, on the
other hand, is not a hard, gregarious view of them
to be equally avoided?

I do not ask to raise them to *more*, but not to

sink them to *less* than men. Our army is no "Corporation without a soul;" it is a mass of units—a collection of beating hearts, throbbing pulses, and straining nerves, which ask and need our love and sympathy, and surely they should not ask in vain.

I have anticipated your question, dear reader, "Why bore us with your conversation with your friend?" Simply because that conversation has led to the further bore of this volume. These notes were jotted down as the incidents occurred; they are a simple statement of facts simply stated. The only object of collecting them at present is that, as my friend's feeling appears to be a general one, it seemed possible that these instances might prove, in some small degree, the converse of the proposition; and, although at any other time quite unworthy of publication, the intense and absorbing desire, at present, to obtain particulars of even the most trifling circumstances connected with the war, has led me to hope that they may not be wholly without interest.

In conclusion, I must regret the necessity of any mention of self; but the nature of the subject requires this, and without it, very frequently the point to be established would be lost. I have

2

omitted many incidents from this very objection, but it would be unjust to the cause which I have at heart to do more, and I must therefore trust that the reader will believe me, when I say that any such allusion arises from necessity, not taste.

AUGUST, 1863.

FLORIAN.—A soldier, didst thou say, Horatio? What! Is't from
the ranks you mean? Faugh!

HORATIO.—Marry, I did! A soldier and a man; and, being a
soldier, all the manlier, maybe.
We "Faugh!" and turn our precious noses to the wind,
As breath from ranks, perforce must be rank breath;
But, mark, my lord, God made the ranks, and more,
God died for those same ranks, as well as men of rank.

OLD PLAY.

(16)

NOTES OF HOSPITAL LIFE.

INTRODUCTION.

LIFE in a hospital! When and where? Now and here. Now, in the year of our Lord one thousand eight hundred and sixty-three; here, in this good city of Philadelphia, whose generous outpouring of her sons, for the cause, nearest all our hearts, can only be matched by the loving tenderness with which she receives and cherishes them, on their return, maimed and mutilated, to their homes amongst us. Every one, who knows anything of the subject at the present moment, is well aware, that no matter where it may be situated, whether opened at the first need, or the creation of yesterday, still "our Hospital" will be, to the speaker, the most perfect in arrangement, discipline, and ventilation; the medical staff connected with it the most efficient, skilful and faithful; the corps of subordinates the most competent, systematic and thorough. Such is human nature, and we all find the weakness a pardonable one.

2 * (17)

How natural it seems to be here! How naturally we accept this strange daily life! And yet, how unnatural it would have seemed two years ago, could we have lifted but one little corner of that mystic veil, which so blessedly prevents even a glimpse of the coming hour; how unnatural, I say, would it have seemed to us, to be standing, as we are at the present moment, in a little domain of our own, consecrated exclusively to us; turning to all sorts of utterly unwonted avocations; any and every sort of service which may bring comfort or aid to those who were strangers to us, till this very day, and after a few to-morrows, will, in all probability, be strangers to us forevermore.

And yet, how glad we are to do it, and they to have it done. "Stop there, my friend," you say. "'And they to have it done.' Is that so? Are the men quite as glad to have it done, as you to do it?" Ah, you have heard that cry. I too have heard it, and will tell you frankly, and as far as possible, impartially, my own conclusion, after careful examination of that point:

"Women are not needed in these hospitals."

"Depend upon it, ladies are a bore here."

"The men are victimized."

All these and many similar remarks have I heard, and they have led me earnestly to look at the question in all its bearings. The petty jealousy of man and his work; the narrowness and littleness of mind

which bristles with indignant anger at the suggestion of man's superiority, are all unworthy of the
great cause we have at heart.   But one question is
before us.   Are the facts so, or are they not?   If,
after every effort honestly to get at the truth, it
shall appear that there really is no need of woman
and her work; that these enormous collections of
suffering and dying human beings, massed together
by this ruthless rebellion, with its wretched results,
actually and positively, may be carried on better,
more practically, more systematically, without her
aid and co-operation, then let her promptly and
decidedly retire; let her do it without anger, without clamor, without bitterness; she is not needed.
If this be so, let her turn into some other channel
the love and tenderness which she longs to lavish
on those who are giving their heart's blood to
defend and protect her.

If this be so, I say; but if on the other hand it
shall appear that her presence is not productive of
disorder; not distasteful to the men; that she is
not only sanctioned, but welcomed by the authori-
ties in charge, then let her go "right onward,"
unmindful of coldness, calumny, or comment from
the world outside, strong in the consciousness of
singleness of aim and purity of purpose.   And,
more than this, if the Dread Day may show, that
through her kneeling at the bedside of one sinning
soul, through her teaching of

> " truths, not ' her's,' indeed,
> But set within ' his' reach by means of ' her,' "

the dark Door of Death has been changed into the
White Gate of Life Everlasting, shall it not then
be granted that women were needed?

This is not the time or place to enter upon the
great question of woman's mission. She has her
work, and the time is coming when she shall be
permitted to do it. God, in His own marvellous
way, is, even now, causing the dawn of that blessed
day to break, when, rising above prejudice and
party spirit, she shall be allowed to take her true
place, and be, in the highest sense of the word, a
"Sister" to the suffering and the sorrowful; to
assert and claim her "rights," the only rights of
which a woman may justly be proud.

> " What are Woman's Rights?"
> " The right to wake when others sleep;
> The right to watch, the right to weep;
> The right to comfort in distress,
> The right to soothe, the right to bless;
> The right the widow's heart to cheer,
> The right to dry the orphan's tear;
> The right to feed and clothe the poor,
> The right to teach them to endure.
>
> " The right when other friends have flown,
> And left the sufferer all alone,
> To kneel that dying couch beside,
> And meekly point to Him who died;
> The right a happy home to make
> In any clime, for Jesu's sake;
> Rights such as these, are all we crave,
> Until our last—a quiet grave."

Anxious, as I have said, to discover whether our presence in the hospital was really acceptable or not, I have closely watched the countenances of the men on the entrance of the lady visitors. I speak not now of myself, for I am merely one, and a most insignificant one, among many; but I can truly say, that at all such times I have never, but once, seen other than an expression of pleasure, and the warm greeting is apparently most sincere. The one instance to which I allude, is certainly no argument against the presence of ladies; it extended to every one who approached his bedside, and was produced by intense physical anguish, acting on a highly nervous organization. I merely name it now, because it is, as I have said, the sole instance in which we were not welcomed and urged to stay. And yet, the very words, in that suffering, pleading tone, "Dear lady, please to go away, I am so very wretched," proved that it was no dislike to us personally, but merely that terrible state, too well known to any one of a very nervous temperament, when even the stirring of the air by the bedside seems a pain. Subsequent events, which I have noted elsewhere, show this to have been the case.

At the time of the visit of the Surgeon-General of the United States to inspect the hospitals, it was rumored, though wholly without foundation, that his object was to change the organization and remove the ladies. The burst of feeling with which this rumor was received was more than gratifying, it was convincing, and proved that if the men were "victimized" they were quite unconscious of it. Only a day or two since, as I was sitting by one of our sick men, M. passed with some preparation in her hand, which she had just made. He turned to me, and pointing to her, said, "I don't think all our angels are in heaven, do you?"

The same feeling, though not always expressed in the same words, seems to be entertained by one and all. "Tell me," said I to one the other day, "if I am in your way?"

"In our way!" said he, "is the green grass in our way?"

"No, for you walk over it, and I have no wish to be trampled on."

He looked disappointed. "I didn't mean that, Miss, I meant its presence always cools and refreshes us, and I thought you'd understand."

"I did quite understand, and thank you," I said, sorry that I had pained him by rejecting the well-meant expression of feeling.

Any one who seriously desires to ascertain the truth, (and to such only do I address myself) will believe that these instances are not recorded for the sake of retailing compliments, but as proofs of a far deeper feeling, which, there can be little doubt, does exist in the hearts of the men amongst whom we are appointed to minister.

OUR DAILY WORK.

AUGUST, 1862.

You ask me, dear C., the usual question, when our work at the hospital is mentioned, " What can the ladies find to do all day?" I might give you the stereotyped answer, " We receive and register the donations, give out and oversee the clothing, make either delicacies or drinks for the men who are ill, read to them, write for them, and try to make ourselves generally useful." This is the ordinary answer, but I think it would be more agreeable to you to come and see for yourself; one day is a pretty good specimen of every day, at least at present, so don your bonnet and jump into the cars with me. What do you say? That the sun is too scorching and the air too heavy for exertion? You think so here, but come with me, and you will soon forget weather and self in more important affairs; at least, so I find it. You agree? Well, then, here we are; why don't you acknowledge the guard's salute as we enter? Shall we pause for a moment in the wards, before we begin our work? I think we had better do so, for in these days, when we once enter our room, there is no escape, while

the light lasts. There are several cases here which
I should like to point out to you as we pass along,
though we cannot give much time to them to-day.
Do you see the man bending over that geranium
plant in the window?   I think I have never seen a
more real, true, deep love of flowers in any one than
in him.   You see how lovingly he leans over that
bush, as though each leaf were a special pet and
darling.   I have often, this summer, brought him
a few roses — as much, I believe, for my own pleasure as his — that I might watch his delight.   He
would sit often for nearly an hour looking at them,
holding them in his hands and lingering over them,
it seemed, with a feeling too deep for words.

I never could tell whether it was pure love of the
flowers themselves, or whether they brought home,
with all its memories, before him; and as he is
very reserved, I content myself with giving the
enjoyment without being too critical as to its cause.

But while I am talking, I see that your eyes are
wandering to that bed, where one of our sickest
men is lying.   He is an Irishman, and far gone in
consumption, poor fellow!   He has interested me
much by his air of silent, weary suffering, and
from his loneliness; he seems to have no friends
anywhere, and is very grateful for the least service
rendered him.   And yet he has a good deal of
drollery about him, and when his pain will let
him, often amuses the men with his dry remarks.

The other day, as I passed him, his hard, hollow cough was followed by such a deep, heavy sigh, that I stopped at once, saying, "What can I do for you, Jones? Is there nothing that you want?"

"Nothing, ma'am, nothing; sure, and what I want, is what you can't give."

"Tell me what it is; perhaps I may be able to help you."

"Sure, and it's lonely I am, so very lonely; and it's some one to love that I'm wanting."

"Ah," said I, "you were right to say I couldn't help you, for unfortunately wives are not provided by Government."

Here his Irish humor gained the ascendant, and with a merry twinkle in his eye, so mournful but a moment before, he said, "But I'm thinking that's jist what you ladies is here for, to supply what isn't provided by Government."

"Exactly," said I, much amused; "but I do not find wives among the list of luxuries on our diet-table. Jones, look at the man at your side, the man opposite to you, and the man directly in front of you; ask each one of those three what is their greatest trouble at this moment, and I happen to know exactly what they will tell you.

"The one at your side is wearying for a letter from his far distant home, which will not come, and dreading that even on its arrival, it will only tell him of sickness and suffering among those dearest to him, and which, lying here, he has no power to relieve; the man opposite to you has just read me a letter from his wife, telling him that she and the children were almost starving; she has hurt her right arm, and can no longer work, scarcely hold the pen to write that letter, and he will send no pay,—charging him with it, as though the poor fellow could help it."

"'God knows,' he says, 'every cent I ever earned was at her service and the weans;' (he is a Scotchman, as I knew, when I heard him say that) 'but the pay don't come, and I lie here thinking all night, till I sometimes feel I must pray very hard or I shall cut my throat.'

"I have been trying to comfort him with the assurance that he will be paid before long, and have been telling him how many difficulties there are in the way of prompt payment in the army, and that the men must try to be patient, and believe that the Government has a hard task, far harder than they know, to meet all the requirements which this sad state of things necessarily causes.

"The man directly in front of you, unable as you know to rise from his bed, has just heard of his wife's death, here in the city, and does not know who will see to her funeral, nor who will take care of his little ones; now, may not some things be worse than loneliness?"

"Faith, an' its truth you're spakin'; a sight worse are such things than all this pain and cough; and I'll think of that same, when the other thought comes, when my breath's so short, and the pain's so bad, that longing to have an old woman to say, 'Is it sufferin' ye are, Jones, dear?' and I'm just the sort to fret, if she was wantin', and I lyin' here, not able to help her. Thank you, ma'am, I see it's far best as it is." And I left poor Jones, convinced that there were circumstances in which an "old woman" was better "in posse," than "in esse."

But what will become of our duties if we linger here so long; let us go now to our room and commence operations. Look before you. Do you know what that barricade at the door means? Three barrels and two large boxes, and they are saying, "Unpack me, unpack me, or there will be nothing left." Do you wonder how I have found out that such are their views? Everything on earth has a mode of its own of conveying ideas; look at the bottom of those barrels, and the floor near those boxes, and you will find that red stream gently flowing there, quite as eloquent and quite as easily understood as any words. That is liquid currant jelly, which, probably, as in a box we opened yesterday, has been of an adventurous turn of mind, one of the Peripatetic school, and not content with the narrow limits to which its friends

have confined it, has burst its bounds, and made
acquaintance with sheets, shirts, and stockings;
and you will soon see a mournful mélange of jelly,
broken glass, and clothing; and fortunate for you
if you do not mingle your own blood with it before
you are done. Do not imagine that all our boxes
have such a sad fate; many arrive in prime order,
but whenever we see that suspicious color at the
bottom of barrels and boxes, we know what to
fear. Only a day or two ago, a large box, containing a dozen and a half large earthenware crocks
of apple-butter, arrived, from which we could only
rescue two, the others being a motley mass of but-
tered earthenware and straw, scarcely a desirable
article for hospital diet. Dear friends in the country! whose generous hearts prompt you to send
delicacies to the sick and suffering soldiers, let me
beg for more careful packing; slats of wood between
the jars would prevent them from falling together,
as they usually do when hurriedly lifted up and
placed on end; we regret the loss as much, or more
than you can do, for we see the disappointment of
the men as they take out one broken piece after
another, and vainly try to separate crockery or
glass from preserves.

Here comes a ready helper. Yes, John, roll them
right into our room, and please bring a hatchet and
open that box for us; I know it's all sticky, but

that can't be helped, we must do the best with it that we can.

And now, while he is taking the lid of the box off for us, and opening the barrels, take a seat and look round you. This is the ladies' room, where we spend so much of our time, and where all our work is done. But first, let me put our kettle on the stove, we must soon begin our cooking; for as I have told you, we prepare the delicacies for the men who are ill; cook eggs for them, stew oysters, make corn-starch, farina, arrow root, or chocolate; don't laugh! yes, even I have found "ignorance" so far from "bliss," that with M.'s valuable instructions, I am really learning to do something useful, incredible as it appears to you. What do you say? That you would not care to test the truth of my statements by taste? Ah well! you shall not be tried, and in the meantime the men are satisfied, which is my only aim. The clothing you see here on the shelves, consists almost entirely of donations. We do not keep the Government clothing here—at least only certain articles — as all the flannel is. drawn by the men and taken from their pay; but we have been so liberally supplied from the different Churches, and from various societies, that it has generally been in our power to give them what they need, and allow them to retain the articles.

" Well, little one, come here, bring me your box, and I will empty it for you. Nice fresh lint, all

3 *

linen, and clean, too; that will be much better
than what you brought before; and now here is
your box; I will tell the poor wounded soldiers
that a kind little girl made it for them; and, goodbye now, run home, for we have so little room here,
and so many things to do, that little girls are only
in the way."

This is only the advance guard of the little army,
which daily, from "morn till dewy eve," keeps
pouring in, company after company,—I might
almost say regiment after regiment,—with their
little boxes or papers of lint, often made of muslin,
and bearing the impress of the little soiled fingers
that picked it. But we always receive it and
thank them. Whether it can be used or not, the
kind intention is the same, and who could have the
heart to refuse the offering of a child? More than
this, the beaming faces and sunny smiles with
which they present it, as though it were some
precious gift, more than atone for the time they
occupy in attending to them.

Turn the key in that closet door, and you will
see all our jellies, preserves, wines, syrups, etc. It
is so full just now, that it was proposed to run up
another room for a donation room, as we really do
not know where to pack away all our things; but
the surgeon tells us, what is very true, that this
cannot last; at the present time there is an unusual
interest and excitement, which can scarcely con-

tinue, and we must take care of these things till
the time of need.   Ah! take care, John! there
goes the top; look into the box; just as I thought;
see, what masses of jelly and broken glass; what
nice fine handkerchiefs, too good for the purpose
by far; carry them straight to the laundry; but
no! that was the way Susan got that bad cut the
other day; bring a pan, and we will let them soak
here first.   Just look at these poor books; with
red edges, indeed, and rubricated throughout; and
writing-paper, too, all soaked with this erratic
currant jelly; and what is this?   A pen; "cur-
rente calamo," indeed, in a new sense.   And these
nice pillow-cases, and towels, and sheets,—but they
can be washed; what is next?   A bundle of——

"My punches ready, miss? for the fourth ward,
ten to-day; here's the Doctor's list."

"Not just yet, Price; you're always in such a
hurry for your men."

"You see, miss, they wouldn't take any breakfast,
and I want something for them."

This from the most faithful and attentive of
wardmasters.   At the beginning of each week, we
receive our orders from the surgeon of each ward
as to how many men need milk punch, extra nourishment, etc.   The wardmaster also has a list, and
his duty is to come to us, get their drinks, and take
them to them; but if there is any delay the ladies
usually take them to the men themselves, that they

may be certain of having them at the proper time. M. kindly undertakes that part of the work to-day, so let us get on with our unpacking.

Let us take out this bundle and see what it is. Enter at this moment three men, each bearing a large market-basket. "These are donations from the —— Society; please let us have the baskets, and an acknowledgment for the things." This sounds trifling, but it means that everything must be taken out, a list made and sent to the Officer of the Day to write an acknowledgment.

Let us do it as quickly as we can; but here comes one of our wardmasters. "Well, Henry, what do you want?"

"Twelve wounded men, ma'am, just come in; the ambulances we were looking for have just got here, and we want a change of clothing for each of them."

"Yes, you shall have them at once, but stand out of Green's way; look what he and William are carrying."

"Green, where did those come from?" Two large boxes of oranges and one of lemons.

"Dr. —— says, miss, these have just been sent, and he would like to have them picked over, as they're spoiling so fast."

"Well, try and find a place for them on the floor, and tell Arnold to come here in a few minutes, and help us to do it."

You may wonder that we do not leave such work entirely to the men, but they understand "picking them over" in the sense of "picking and stealing;" and I am afraid that unless we assisted there would be few left for the sick when the work was done. The men are always ready and glad to help us in anything that we allow them to do; indeed, I have often been surprised at the promptness with which they offer their services to spare us in every way; to carry and empty water for us, to run our errands, to watch our fire; in short, to render any little service which is most needed at the moment, and which we should naturally do for ourselves, unless the offer were made.

Enter a group of women—I humbly beg their pardon—ladies, I should have said. Ah! I know too well their errand before they speak. Persons have been coming all the week for the same purpose.

"Can we see the rebel? Please to show us the ward where the rebel is confined?"

"I am sorry, ladies, but it is quite impossible——"

"Eight punches for our ward, Miss ——, are they ready?"

"Yes, Williams, standing on the shelf there; take them on that waiter."

"The surgeon in charge has given strict orders that no visitors are to be admitted to that ward,

as there are some men dangerously ill there, and
he wishes it kept perfectly quiet."

" But we've come a great way to see him, and
we must get in."

"Are you friends of his ? If so, I will see the
surgeon about it."

" Friends of a rebel ! Not exactly, thank you.
We want to see what he's like."

" I am sorry, but you cannot see him. However,
I can assure you that he is exactly like any of
these men you see around you; were you to go
into the ward you could not distinguish him, unless
he were pointed out to you."

Enter a man, with a large glass bowl of jelly.

" Mrs. ——'s compliments, and please give me
the bowl to take back."

Mem. Jelly to be emptied; nothing to empty
it into. During the search, gloomy party gaze
moodily upon the operation, but show no signs of
departure.

" Brown says, ma'am, you promised to poach
him a couple of eggs for his dinner; he sent me
to see if they were done."

" It is not dinner time yet; tell him they shall be
ready when he hears the drum tapped."

" Have you a flannel shirt, miss, for this man?'
he's just come in."

Look at the indignant party; they are evidently
returning to the assault.

" Where's the head doctor? He'll let us in, we'll see if he won't!"

" The Surgeon in charge is not here at present; the Officer of the Day is in the office; you must have seen him when you were admitted."

" Oh, yes! not him; some friends told us to ask for the ladies; that's the way we got in; we knew they kept the rebel so close, no use to ask for him."

A woman with a basket of eggs.

" Some eggs from Mrs. ——; please let me have the basket."

" Yes, and thank Mrs. —— for her kindness; she never forgets us, and her nice fresh eggs are most acceptable to the sick men. And now, indeed we must hurry, and put some of this mass of things in their places on the shelves; for this table will be wanted, after dinner, for the donations from the schools; it is the time when they pour in."

" Does he eat with the others?" Supposed to refer to the rebel, and answered accordingly.

" Yes, madam, at the common dining-table."

" Does he talk much?"

" That I cannot inform you, as I have never exchanged a word with him."

" Do they treat him kindly?"

" Precisely as the other men are treated."

"And you think we can't see him?"

" It is quite impossible, for the reasons I have mentioned."

"Well, Jane, there's no use waiting; come along;
I heard there was one at the —— hospital; let's
go there and try." Discomfited party depart
abruptly.

I am glad that you should see this for yourself;
otherwise I think you would hardly credit my
statement, that this has not happened only once
or twice, but literally every day this week, with
different parties, and variations in the modes of
trying to gain admittance. It is indeed difficult
to account for this morbid curiosity with regard
to the Southern prisoners. I have sometimes
thought that it might be an unconscious tribute
to loyalty, and that the crime of rebellion was
looked upon as such a fearful one, that it must
of necessity affect even the external appearance
of all engaged in it; be that as it may, I do most
sincerely believe that were Du Chaillu himself to
hold an exhibition here of one of his Gorillas, it
would attract less attention than the presence
of this one poor misguided rebel. There! while
I have been moralizing upon rebels and the rebellion, don't you think I have given that shelf
rather a neater appearance, and that the table is
beginning to look a little less loaded; but oh. dear!
look at this box at the door; what more is coming?
Oh! I see what it is. I know well that box by
the flag painted on the top. Kind friends from
the country send us that; we have a duplicate

key; empty and return it to have it filled and sent to us next week. The contents are most acceptable, but as you see, it must be attended to at once, and as exactly this work will go on till night, I think you have had quite enough of it, and had better say goodbye to us and our room. This day, just as you have seen it, is a counterpart of every day, not only of this week, but of the last three months. It will not, of course, continue; but, although we would be the last to check the generosity of warm-hearted friends, it makes our duties here a little arduous just at present.

And now let me go with you to the door, and say goodbye. If you find that you are not too much wearied, I shall hope for another visit, in some future week, when I may have time to take you through the wards, and I can show you some of our interesting cases; but I think what you have seen to-day, will furnish the best answer I could give to your question, " What can the ladies find to do there, all day ?"

4

A MORNING AT THE HOSPITAL.

"God's finger touched him, and he slept."

A STEADY, pouring rain. The fog, which in the early morning hesitated whether to roll off and give us one of those beautiful, bright autumn days, the more precious because we feel they are gliding so rapidly from us, or to come down in rain, seems to have decided at last, and a dreary, drenching rain is the result. As we * enter the hospital, a glance is sufficient to tell that some depressing influence is at work; instead of the bright, happy laugh which so often astonishes us on our entrance, we see the men hanging listlessly and languidly round; some grouped in a corner of the dining-room round a piano, which a few generous hearts have supplied for their amusement; some trying a game of cards or back-gammon; others lying on benches, "chewing the cud of sweet and bitter fancies," the latter class having the ascendancy, to

---

* Let me say here, once for all, that the term "we" is not used as the petty affectation of authorship, but is formed by the Lady Visitor with whom I am associated,—the "M." of these pages—whose untiring self-sacrifice, and whole-souled devotion to the cause, can only be appreciated by those whose pleasure it is to be connected with her in this work.

judge from the countenance. Nor is the scene
brighter in the wards; the damp air has driven
those suffering from rheumatism and fever to their
beds once more; and after the first bright smile of
welcome, which never fails to greet us, the words,
"Poor William there, is dying!" are sufficient to
account for the depression, without waiting for
what follows, "and I expect I shall go next."

It is often asserted that the sight of such constant suffering and death, so hardens and accus-
toms the men to the fact, that they do not appear
to feel it in the slightest degree. My own observation has led to a directly opposite conclusion.
It is only natural, that a death here, where every
trace of it is necessarily so speedily removed, may
and must be as speedily forgotten; but, at the time,
I have always noticed a far greater effect from it
than I could have looked for; greater respect and
sympathy for the feelings of any relations present;
greater solemnity in witnessing the awful change;
greater tenderness in the subsequent care of the
body. As an illustration, it was but yesterday,
that one of the wardmasters, coming for a shirt
to lay out one of our poor fellows, just dead, said,
"Give me any one, one of the worst will do," and
then, as though the words struck a chord, he added
instantly; "One of the worst! Oh! how sorry I
am, I said that; poor fellow! poor fellow! he
wouldn't have said that for me;" and as I turned,

I saw the rough arm in its red flannel shirt, brush-
ing away a tear, of which he surely need not have
been ashamed.

"Poor William is dying." Yes, too truly. We
need not the words of the Surgeon in charge, as
he passes, "Don't trouble him with that poultice, it
is too late;" one glance is sufficient; and yet as I
approached the bed I started involuntarily. The
man had only been here a short time, and had
never seemed in any way remarkable; of small
size, very ordinary appearance, light hair, blue
eyes, and a quiet, gentle manner. He had not
been considered in danger, though suffering from
an attack of acute bronchitis; for in this war
truly may it be said,

> "Manifold
> And dire, O Sickness! are the crucibles
> Wherein thy torturing alchemy assays
> The spirit of man."

But now,— could it be the same? I looked at
name and number to satisfy myself. I have no
wish to exaggerate, but *transfigured* was the word
which rose to my mind then, and whenever I have
since thought of that face. The wonderful change
seemed already to have passed upon the spirit,
which looked forth from those large, clear, blue
eyes, double their usual size, as with an eager,
wistful gaze they were evidently fixed upon a
vision too bright for our earth-dimmed sight, while
a smile, a radiant smile, played round his lips. It

was not the poor Private, dying afar from friends
and home, alone in a ward of a hospital, with the
pitiless rain pelting overhead; it was a soul passing
from earth, resting on its dear Lord, strengthened
and comforted for the dread journey by a vision
of the Guard of Angels sent to bear it to its rest
in Paradise; the unearthly peace, the blessed brightness of that face, could not be mistaken.

> "Death upon his face
> Is rather shine than shade."

The doctor's hand is on his pulse, sustaining
stimulants are steadily given, and once more a
fitful gleam of life appears; he rallies for the
moment. We hear the low voice of the chaplain,
kneeling at his side, "You would not object to a
prayer?" The wandering eyes say more than the
languid lips, which can but frame, in a tone of
surprise, the word, "object?" The same bright
smile, the same far-off gaze as the words of prayer
ascend.

"You are trusting, you are resting on the merits
of your precious Saviour?"

Once more that strife, that sore struggle to
speak; and suddenly, as though the will had
mastered the flesh, sounds forth, in clear, strong
tones, which ring through the ward, "My only
base, my foundation!" Blessed for us all, when
that awful hour is upon us, if we can so trustfully,

4 *

so fearlessly meet it; so fully and entirely realize the One Eternal Rock to be our "foundation."

We dare no longer call him "poor William;" rather, as we kneel by his side, let us breathe forth a thanksgiving for such beautiful assurance, that his last battle is fought, his victory won.

> "Little skills it when or how,
> If Thou comest then or now—
> With a smooth or angry brow.

> "Come Thou must, and we must die—
> Jesu, Saviour, stand Thou by,
> When that last sleep seals our eye!"

THE TWO ARMIES.

U. S. A. HOSPITAL, September 29, 1862.

I TRUST, dear C., this bright, beautiful day may have brought you as much pleasure as it has done to me, and that you have been able to enjoy it as you would most wish to do. I escaped from my duties here for one hour, and spent it you know where. On my return, we were favored with a visit from the Bishop of Minnesota, who is here on his way to the General Convention.

He seemed much interested in going through the wards, had a kind word and friendly greeting for each man. One thing particularly impressed me,—his tact in addressing them. Instead of boring them as I do with " What is your name ? What is your regiment ?" he glanced his eye upon the card at the head of the bed, whereon all such particulars are written, and then said, " Who is the colonel of the Forty-fourth ?" or, " Was the Eighteenth Massachusetts much cut up ?" Instantly the man would brighten, feel that there was one who took a personal interest, and answer with promptness and pleasure.

This may seem a trifle, but to gain an influence

anywhere trifles must be considered, and are often
all-important. My inward exclamation was, immediately, "Here is one who has been accustomed
to dealing with men, and knows how to reach
them." A few well-chosen questions will often
go further, and be of more benefit, than a long
sermon.

As you have expressed some interest in L——,
you will forgive·me for repeating a conversation
to which this visit gave rise. A little later, I
returned for some purpose to his bedside.

"That's a nice man you brought here; what
was it you called him?"

"The title I gave him," said I, "he gained by
promotion in our Army."

"Our army! I knew it, by the way he talked;
then he's a volunteer?"

"Yes."

"Ever been in a battle?"

"Many of them."

"Wounded?"

"Often."

"That's bully. But what battles? Fair Oaks?
That's where I was hit."

"He never told me so, but I should judge his
hardest fights were before the breaking out of this
rebellion."

"Ah, in Mexico?"

"No, I never heard of his being in Mexico."

"A foreigner?"

"No, I believe him to be an American."

"It can't be, then, for he looks too young for our other war. Didn't he tell you what battles?"

"No, he never told me, nor did any of his friends."

"Then how the ——, I beg ten thousand pardons, miss, but how can you know he was in them?"

"Because it is my privilege to be a Private in the same Army. I said *our* Army was the one in which he had gained promotion; and It's peculiarity is, that It will receive as recruits both women and children."

Impossible as it may appear to you, he fixed his eyes upon me with an air of bewilderment, and remained perfectly silent. I continued:

"Although I am not eligible for promotion as he is, but must remain a Private always, I have had some of the same battles to fight, and——"

"Psha! you've been fooling me all this time, and I never saw it."

I smiled. "Not fooling," I said, "but answering a question you asked the other day. Have you forgotten when you said 'Little you know of battles!' that I replied, 'And yet, maybe, I have fought harder ones than you ever did?' You then asked me what under the sun I could mean? I promised to tell you. and I have only done so in a round-about way. Have you forgotten one thing more? What was it I asked you to give up, when you said you had rather be shot?"

His color rose, but he said nothing.

"Doesn't that prove that my battles, and those of that 'nice man,' as you term the bishop, are harder to fight than yours?"

"Well, it's truth you're saying; I'd liever go back to my regiment to-morrow, wounded as I am, than do what you want, though I know you're right, too;" and warmly shaking my hand, he drew the cover over his head, and I left him to meditate upon the two Armies.

You will say that the strain after originality in such conversations, is not likely to be an over-tax of the mental powers; but you must remember, that what to you may be but a wearying platitude, may be a seed, to one who receives the parallel as a novelty, to germinate in later years.

We can but try all means, and leave events to God.

THE CONTRAST.

"I wish to goodness they would not send their men here, just to die!"

Such was the exclamation, in no very amiable tone, which greeted my ear, as I opened the door of one of the wards of our hospital.

"What is the matter, Wilson?" said I, to our usually cheerful wardmaster.

"Oh! nothing, miss; I beg your pardon, only there's a young fellow, just brought in, who, the doctor thinks, can't live over the day, and I hate to have them dying on my hands, that's all."

"Wounded or sick?"

"It's the typhoid, and as bad a case as ever I saw yet, and I've seen a heap of them, too. There he is, but he's past speaking; he'll never rouse again."

I approached the bed, where lay a "young fellow," truly: a boy, scarcely more than sixteen; his long, thick hair matted and tangled; his clothing torn and soiled; his eyes half closed; his lips dark and swollen; a bright flush on his cheeks, and his breath coming in quick, short, feverish pantings, as though much oppressed. I saw it was quite in vain to speak to him, and merely tried to make him swallow the beef tea, which had been ordered to be given him at certain intervals.

He swallowed with much difficulty, but still it was something that he could do even this; and I found that although unable to speak, he understood and endeavored to obey, directions. I therefore ventured to doubt Wilson's verdict, and continued to administer the stimulants as directed. Towards afternoon there was a perceptible improvement in his swallowing; he roused partially, and attempted to turn. I begged Wilson to watch him closely through the night, keeping up the nourishment and stimulants; urging as a motive that, as he wasn't fond of deaths, this was the best mode of preventing them.

He shook his head. "I'll watch him as close as you could, miss, but it's no use. I've seen too many cases to think that poor lad can weather thro' it; I reckon you're new to this sort of thing, or you would know it too."

"Did you ever hear a saying, Wilson, 'Duties are ours, events are God's?' Try, I only ask you to try."

The next morning, when I walked in, I scarcely recognized our patient; in addition to clean clothing, combed and cut hair, his eyes were open, large, bright, and sparkling with a feverish brilliancy.

He was talking in a loud, excited tone; evidently the stupor had passed off; whether a favorable change, or denoting increase of fever, I was not competent to decide.

As I drew near, I was a little startled by the abrupt question, "Are you the woman gave me the drinks yesterday?"

I assented, sure that no discourtesy was intended by the use of the good old Anglo-Saxon term. Strange, that by some singular freak of language or ideas, which, I think, it would puzzle even the learned Dean of Westminster himself to explain, this once honored title has, at the present day, come to be almost a term of reproach; certainly, as I have said, of discourtesy. Were this the place to moralize, I might see in this change a proof of the degeneracy of modern days; and question, whether in yielding this precious name,— sacred forever, and ennobled by the use once made of it, —Woman is not in danger of yielding also the high and noble qualities which should ever be linked with its very sound.

My assent was followed instantly by another equally abrupt question, "Then you'll tell me where do people go when they die? That man, there—I heard him—said I was dying; I've been asking him all night, and he won't tell me."

"If you will mind what I say now, and try to

5

be very still, when you have less fever, I will talk
to you and tell you all you want to know."

"I'll be dead then, and I want to know before
I die."

Very sure that any excitement at present must
be injurious, after several ineffectual attempts to
divert his mind, I deemed it best to leave him,
making an excuse of other duties, and promising
to return if he would try to keep quiet. The surgeon's report was favorable; the change in him
was quite unexpected, and recovery was possible,
though by no means probable.

I left him alone, purposely, for some hours; but
the moment I re-entered the ward he exclaimed,
"Now you will tell me."

Judging it better to quiet his mind, I sat down
and spoke to him quietly and gently of his home.
Home! the talisman which charms away all pain
and soothes all sorrow. Should any one ask how
to reach the men? how gain an influence over
them? I would reply by pointing them to Na-
poleon's policy, or later, to our own Burnside,
and let the fields of Roanoke and Newbern bear
witness to the success of the experiment. Attack
the centre. Storm the heart. Make a man speak
of his home. Listen, while he tells with bitter
self-reproach, how he enlisted without consent;
and how, since then, the night wind's wail seems
mourning mother's moan; listen to the tearful

tale of the loneliness of some brave-hearted wife, who sent her treasure forth, and battles nobly on at home; (which is the harder strife?) or of the parting hour, and clinging clasp of little arms round that rough neck, which would not be undone, and which may never tighten there again.   And once more listen, as I did yesterday, to an account of a return home, on a furlough, of one bronzed and weather-beaten by severe service and exposure; the joyful expectation; the journey; the gradual approach to the well-known gate; every detail dwelt upon and lingered over; "And, if you'll believe it, my Charlie didn't know me! I couldn't stand it nohow;" and the tears which will not be repressed, fall thickly on the crutches at his side. Lead a man, I say, to tell you such things as these, and he can never again feel towards you as a stranger; he will bring you his letters, or tell you their contents, with a feeling that you know the persons therein mentioned, and will sympathize with either his joy or sorrow.   The citadel is won; he has put the key into your hands which you may fit at any moment to the lock of his heart, and enter at will; thus is a bond established between you, for the proper improvement of which you will be responsible in the sight of God.

But this victory, like many another we have won, is a very partial one; the fortress may be gained, but the difficulty is to hold it, and garrison

it with the troops that we would fain see there.
Golden Charity, the commander-in-chief of our
forces, has had, and will yet have, many a weary
battle to wage, ere She can obtain even a foothold
in such unwonted quarters; but with the all-important aid of Her staff officers, Faith and Hope,
we look for final success, even though we may not
be permitted to see it.

But do not imagine that poor Ennis has been the
victim of this digression. After a few moments'
conversation, the eager, excited tone died away,
and he told me quietly that he had been brought
up in "the woods of Jersey;" had driven a team
there, and worked on a farm; spoke of his ignorance with pain; the great grief seemed to be
that he could not read; if he should live, wouldn't
I teach him?

"Nobody never taught me nothing; will God
mind, if I should die?"

"Did your mother never teach you your letters?"

"She don't know 'em herself."

A little more talk, and the sentences became
broken, the words disconnected, and ere long I
left him in a natural, comfortable sleep.

He suffered terribly from pain in his head, and
the doctor had forbidden all unnecessary noise in
the ward. I was therefore not a little surprised
the next morning as I approached the door, to
hear loud, noisy singing, laughing and talking

alternately, such as I had never at any time heard since I had visited the hospital.

I paused at the door, hesitating to enter, and knowing the state in which I had left Ennis, both provoked and indignant. Just at that moment, one of the orderlies came out, and to my question as to the meaning of the disturbance, informed me that a new case of violent fever and delirium had just been brought in, and as the other wards were crowded, it had been a necessity to place him here. Thus re-assured, I walked in, when Wilson at once came up to me with, " Oh, Miss —— if you would only try. This man's out of his head—he can't live—and the doctor ordered us to find out where his friends are, if possible, and let them know. He has a good deal of money in his knapsack, and we should like to know what to do with it; if his friends are far off, they couldn't be here in time, but we can't tell."

" Has he had no intervals of consciousness?" I asked, not caring to show how I shrank from the task.

" None, and he won't have till he goes into a stupor, and then the game's up."

I was too much worried at the time to ask whether an "interval of consciousness" was supposed to exist during a stupor, as his words seemed to imply, and merely said,

5 *

"But if you have tried in vain, what object is there in my speaking to him?"

As I spoke, a burst of noisy, insane laughter came from his lips, and rang discordantly through the ward; he tried to spring from his bed, but was forcibly held on each side.

"Perhaps it's no good, miss, but it seemed our last chance, and if you'd just try?"

Here was a trial. And yet, had I enlisted only for sunny weather? Was I to shrink at the first chance of service? Nevertheless, I did shrink, and, I fear, very visibly, too; but I felt I must go forward, or deserve to be stricken from the rolls. Could the exact springs of all our actions be known, I fear it would too often be seen that they arise in many cases from motives which we should be most unwilling to confess; so in this case, I sincerely believe that it was the shame of uttering the simple truth "I am afraid of him," which led me straight to his bedside, far more than the benevolent wish of informing distant relatives of his dying condition.

"Have you ever heard him mention any of his family at any time?" said I to Wilson, as we crossed the ward, half to keep him with me, and half to know how to address this dreaded, wild-looking creature.

"Yes, he did say something once about a sister,

but if we ask him anything further, he bursts out singing or laughing, and it's no use."

The power of the eye I had frequently heard of, and also that a single, direct question, often steadies the unbalanced mind. I could but try them now. I had an indistinct impression, as I drew near, that it would be easier to face the hottest fire of the fiercest foe in the field, than the glare of those eyes; but, trying to look at him steadily, I said, slowly and distinctly,

"What is your sister's name?"

He looked at me for a moment, surprised and perfectly silent, and then, to my utter amazement, replied with equal distinctness, "Susanna Weaver."

"Where does she live?"

"Westchester, Pennsylvania."

This was so evidently a success, that I ventured further, though doubtful of the result.

"How do you direct your letters?" No hesitation,

"Mrs. Susanna Weaver, care of James Weaver, shoemaker, Westchester, Pennsylvania."

As he uttered the last word, a man who had just come in, came up to me.

"What he says, ma'am, ain't no use; he's out of his head, and he don't mean it."

I said nothing in reply, but was satisfied as to the truth of my own conclusions, when, two days afterwards, I walked in to see the veritable Susanna, wife of James Weaver, shoemaker, portly, patronizing, and polite, fanning her apparently insensible brother, and applying ice to his temples, for the dreaded stupor had come on.

My poor Ennis lay for a long time in a low, exhausted state; but the doctor gave hope, and at length he began perceptibly to improve. His eagerness to be taught — more especially upon religious subjects—continued; there was something so simple and childlike about him; so touching in the terror which he felt with regard to death; so winning in his weakness, so gentle in his goodness, or his aims after it, that I could not help becoming deeply interested in him. He knew that there was a God—a Being to be dreaded in his view—a Life after death; beyond this — nothing. Our blessed Lord's life and death, His work on earth, His giving His life for us, all seemed new and strange ideas which he could with difficulty grasp. Never can I forget the intense interest with which he followed me, step by step, through the dark and dread story of The Last Week; I almost feared the excitement which burned in his eager eyes, till, as I closed, his pent-up feelings found vent in the words, "It was too bad!" His powers of language were limited, not so his powers of feeling; and I imagine that we, to whom that mighty mystery is so familiar from childhood, can scarcely conceive its effect when heard for the first time.

He took perfect delight in hearing and learning
the prayers from the Prayer-book, and would ask
for them constantly. And here I must speak of
the wonderful power which seems to live, in the
short, terse nature of our matchless Collects, to
stay a weak and wandering mind; "the soul by
sickness all unwound" cannot bear many words;
but the concentration of devotion, in many of
those short, earnest sentences, seems to meet every
longing and to supply every want. As Ennis so
greatly needed instruction, at my request a clergy-
man, who had frequently visited the hospital, and
whose ministrations were always peculiarly acceptable to the men, came often and spent much
time with him.* At one time, when I was not on
duty, he sent for me. "Why did you want me,
Ennis, the ladies who are here are so very kind
to you, and do everything you can want?"

"Not you, but I do so want that pretty prayer
you know." The "Prayer for a sick person" from
our Prayer-book. I doubt whether any one was
ever more gratified, by being told that they were
not wanted personally, but merely for what they
could bring.

I must return here, for a little while, to my old
friend, whose delirium and stupor, to the wonder

* This was, of course, before the Government appointment of our
present faithful and efficient Chaplain, whose earnest and self-denying
labors render any such service quite needless.

alike of physicians and nurses, passed off, after
many weeks of tedious suffering, during which
time I had talked to him, read to him, and written
letters at his dictation, quite unconscious that he
was still very much under the influence of fever.
His sister remained till she saw that he would
probably live, and then was obliged to return to
her home. He could carry on a perfectly rational
conversation, although always inclined to excitement; and it was quite evident, from the whole
tone of his remarks, that his "hoary hairs" were
anything but a "crown of righteousness." I link
these two cases together because they were so
linked, strangely enough, from the beginning, and
still more in the end, and so must ever remain in
my mind.

Several weeks passed by, during which I was
not at the hospital; and when I returned, what
was my surprise to find our patient up, dressed,
and seated by the stove. "Why, Jackson, is it
possible? How glad I am to see you so much
better."

He looked at me without a sign of recognition,
rose, bowed, but said nothing.

"Don't you remember me, or what is the matter?" said I, thoroughly puzzled.

"I never saw you before, ma'am, did I? Never
to my knowledge."

"Well done for you, Jackson!" and "That's a

good one, isn't it?" burst from more than one
of the men, with a hearty laugh.

He looked troubled and bewildered. I saw the
whole thing at once. "Never mind, Jackson,"
said I, "you have been very ill,—as ill as it was
possible to be to recover, and you remember nothing of that time; I suppose it seems like a long
dream."

Such was precisely the case. Even the weeks
when I had supposed him perfectly conscious, were
all a blank; he had not the slightest recollection
even of being brought in, and of nothing afterwards until the weeks during which I had been
away.

My pale, attenuated boy, too, was changed into
the round, ruddy young soldier, looking particularly well in his uniform. As is so frequently the
case in typhoid fevers, he had gained flesh rapidly,
as he recovered, and felt all the buoyancy and
brightness of a thorough convalescence. I could
not avoid comparing and contrasting the two
cases. Both brought in with the same disease;
in the same apparently hopeless state; the same
surprise excited by the recovery of each; but here
the parallel ceased. The one, scarcely more than
a child,—a beardless boy, with smooth, polished
brow, rising with all the vigor of youth from this
terrible illness, and throwing off the disease as
completely as though it had never touched him.

The other, worn and scarred by life's conflicts
more than by time; his brow deeply furrowed
more by excess than years; his hair prematurely
whitened, rising, it is true, from the disease, but
how?—without spirit, energy, or any sort of spring;
wearily dragging one foot after the other; listlessly
and languidly sitting hour after hour upon his bed,
scarcely noticing or speaking to any one. His
time of life would of necessity give a slower convalescence, but there was far more against him
than this: a constitution broken and ruined, as
we soon found, by bad habits, which he renewed as
soon as permitted to go out, producing, of course,
a relapse. Long before I knew this, I was conscious that I could never overcome my repugnance
to the man; at first I attributed the feeling to the
extreme dread of him I had felt at our first meet-
ing, and which I could not forget; but I soon
became convinced that there was a stronger reason.
If inward purity writes itself upon the outward
form, (and who can question that it does?) the
converse is equally true. There is a sort of instinct, or rather—for that is too low a term—a sort
of spiritual consciousness, which warns us when
evil is near; that part of our being puts forth
feelers, as it were, moral antennæ, which extend
themselves in congenial soil, but recoil at the
touch of corruption of any sort.

Ennis soon brought me a spelling-book, given

him by one of the men, and claimed my promise
to teach him to read. Most faithfully he studied,
but just as we were priding ourselves upon our
progress, and he was triumphantly mastering the
mysteries of "It is he," "I am in," the order came,
and by a strange chance, Jackson and he were to
go on to Washington together, to rejoin their
different regiments. This I exceedingly regretted,
as I looked upon Jackson as very far from a desirable companion or example for a young boy
like Ennis. This feeling was confirmed, when, on
the morning of their departure, Jackson came to
bid me goodbye, with unsteady step and bloodshot
eye. I spoke as I felt, strongly and sternly, as I
could not but feel towards one so lately raised
from the very gate of death, and thus requiting
the Love and Mercy which had spared him. I
know not, and it matters not what I said, but when
I spoke of the fearful responsibility which would
rest upon his soul, should he lead that child committed to his care into sin, he looked surprised
and startled, and promised me, in the most solemn
manner, that he should come to no evil through
him. It would have eased my heart of a heavy
load, could I have relied more implicitly upon that
promise; but, after all, such feelings are but a want
of Faith; because the visible guard was the last
that I should have chosen for him. I forgot that
that young boy went forth attended by a bright,

6

unseen Guard, to guide and protect him through
every step of his way.   And so we parted. Weeks
have formed themselves into months, and months
have formed themselves into a year, but I have
never heard of them, or even seen their names,
and cannot tell whether they are numbered among
the living or the dead.

I can scarcely tell why it is, but there are no
cases, in all the memories of hospital life, which
stand out so clearly stereoscoped upon my brain,
as the two of which I have just spoken.

BROWNING.

THIS morning, as I opened the door of the ladies' room at the hospital, I found M., as usual, before me at her post busily working. She greeted me with "Mr. —— (our chaplain) has just been in, to say that Browning is to be baptized this morning, and he would like us to be present; so we shall have to be prompt with our work."

This Browning was a striking instance of the mercy and long-suffering of our dear Lord and Master. After a wholly irreligious life, he had entered the army, (though quite advanced in years,) at the breaking out of the rebellion, where, instead of being struck down by a bullet, a long and suffering illness in the hospital had been graciously granted to him; it had borne its fruit, and this day, the brow furrowed by sin, and the hair whitened in the service of another master, are to be moistened by baptismal waters.

He has been perfectly blind for many days, and is evidently sinking. At the appointed hour we gather around his bed, the Chaplain, the Surgeon in charge, (whose presence and interest in the occasion impress the men far more than he ima-

gines,) M., and myself. The holy words are pronounced, and he is enlisted as "Christ's faithful
soldier and servant unto his life's end;" that end,
which, alas! seems so very near. As we approach
to speak to him, he looks up, no longer with the
blank, vacant gaze of sightless eyes, which he has
worn for so many days, but with a bright smile
of recognition, saying, in a tone almost of surprise,
"Friends, dear friends, God has given me light."
I thought he alluded to the light which had just
dawned upon his spirit, but not so; it seemed as
though the inward illumination had indeed extended to his physical frame; sight was restored
to the darkened eye of the body also, and mercifully continued during the few remaining days of
his life. To the many, this fact will appear a
strange coincidence; to the few, something more.

Scarcely has the closing prayer ascended; scarcely
have we turned to leave the bedside, when there is
a bustle—an excitement—a sudden stir. "A man
dying in the third ward; come quickly, come, won't
you?"

We hasten to the spot, and to our surprise find
that the Angel of Death is before us. A man, whom
we had been watching for some time, ill with that
terrible scourge — the Chickahominy fever — and
whom we had left not half an hour since, apparently in no danger, by some strange change is
suddenly and certainly dying. His sister, who has

been watching him, night and day, had left him to prepare some drink for him; in her absence he had attempted to rise from his pillow; the effort was too much, and he had, as she imagined, fainted.

But to any eye, whose sad lot it has been to watch that dark, cold, grey shadow, once seen, never forgotten, marvellous in its mystery, strange in its stern solemnity, as it slowly settles on some loved face; to any ear, that has listened to those long, convulsive breaths, with their longer and more dreadful intervals, it could not but be evident that this was no fainting, but the terrible sundering of soul and body. Man's hand here was powerless. In answer to the sister's agonized appeal to the surgeon, brandy is offered, but in vain; and we stand silently and sadly waiting till the dread struggle shall be ended. And still we stand, and still we wait. It seems as though something held and chained the soul to earth; it cannot part —it cannot burst its earthly case.

One by that bed whispers to the chaplain —
"The Last Prayer."

We kneel once more, and once more the wonderful words of the Prayer-book speak for us in our hour of need. It is enough. The cord is broken —the chain is loosed; the soul seems to rise upon the wings of those solemn words; for ere they are done, a broken-hearted sister feels that she is alone.

It is not desirable to enter upon any description

6 *

of the sorrowful scene of excited and undisciplined grief which followed; three hours afterwards, we succeeded in inducing her to take an anodyne and go to bed. Character, mental training, and spiritual attainment, are never more clearly shown than in the manner in which a great sorrow is borne; much, of course, depends upon temperament, but as a rule, I think we may safely affirm, that the most violent outward expression has the least inward root; that the griefs which crush and slowly sap life, are seldom noisily and vehemently vented in their first freshness.

That night, as I sat where the soft shadows of summer moonlight played peacefully in and out among grand old trees, my thoughts naturally clung to the scenes through which I had been passing, and dwelt upon those two who had both, though so differently, that day " entered into Life;" the one, through the Golden Gate of Baptism; the other, through " the grave and gate of death;" and in the calmness of that still night, the fervent wish arose, that they might both attain a "joyful resurrection, for His merits, Who died, and was buried, and rose again for us."

THE TWO ANGELS.

U. S. A. HOSPITAL, August, 1862.

'Tis a hospital ward, and the sun's cheerful rays
  Light up many a bed of pain,
As the sufferers, seeking so sadly for ease,
  Turn wearily once and again.

A small group is gathered round one of the beds,
  Come with me, and stand by its side,
Whilst the voice of the Priest softly sounds on the air
  As he pours the Baptismal tide

By pillows supported, in sore strife for breath,
  See one enter that Army within;
Whose Captain accepts all the maim'd and the halt,
  Whose service is no worth to Him.

O, wonderful Mercy, unspeakable Love!
  Who gave all His best for our sake;
The few faded fragments and dregs of lost life,
  When offered, at latest, will take.

Holy words are pronounced, and his brow with wet Cross,
  Is sparkling with strange, wondrous light;
Whence comes It? We see by that awe-stricken face
  That no longer, as erst, is it night.

There are moments in life, when, from earthly thoughts freed,
  To our sight purer vision is given;
Can we doubt that bright Presence—the Angel of Life—
  As It floats thro' the air, is from Heaven?

White Wings are extended—no poet's mere dream—
  But truly protecting that head;
And the Peace, passing earth, settles soft on our souls,
  As we kneel by that hospital bed.

A bustle, a noise and a crowd, and a stir!
  Some one's dying! oh! come quickly, come!
We hasten, but Man may not stay that Dread Hand,
  With its summons so swift to his Home.

The Angel of Death hovers close o'er the bed;
　The shadow falls dark on the face;
And a chill and a hush rests on everything round,
　Each man standing still in his place.

Yet still the soul lingers, earth bound, as it seems,
　Till a voice whispers low, "The Last Prayer;"
And those words—those grand words of our Mother, The Church—
　Rise clearly and calm on the air.

It seems as they rise, to Faith's eye, thro' the space
　A path for the soul they have cleft;
For we know, ere Amen's last vibration is done,
　With the body alone we are left.

In the wards of Life's Hospital, thus are the threads,
　Of Death and of Life intertwined;
Grant, Lord, in our hour of need, that our souls
　Such vision of Angels may find!

BROWN.

"Alas, long-suffering and most patient God,
Thou need'st be surelier God to bear with us,
Than even to have made us!"

"How you can endure that man, is a mystery to me," said M., to me one morning, as, in going through the wards, I paused at the bedside of one of the men, whose unattractive, even repulsive countenance fully justified the feeling. I did not answer what was the truth, " I cannot endure him," for I had resolved on testing to the uttermost, my theory, most firmly held, that there is some good in every one—some key to the heart—some avenue by which the soul may be reached—some smoulder-ing spark of good in darkest depths of evil; and more than this, we were not there to choose inter-esting cases, but to minister to all. Truly there was little room here for the romantic interest with which we are charged with investing our men. Originally of very low origin, bad habits, probably increased by the exposure of camp life, had sunk him lower; and I confess to a feeling of shame at the unconquerable disgust with which I approached him; but he was sick and suffering, and I tried to fix my mind upon the fact, rather than upon the cause which had produced it.

Several months of visiting, however, proved one point, that he certainly had a heart; further than this, I could not ascertain, even after many trials, until one morning he turned to me, suddenly, and said, pointing to the wall opposite his bed, "We have a light all night; I can't sleep, and I'm all the time reading that." I looked, and read the text in large letters, "There is more joy in heaven, over one sinner that repenteth," &c. "Do you think there could ever be *joy* over me?" The utter depression of the look, the hopelessness of the tone, and the mournful shake of the head, were touching in the extreme.

He seemed to long to do better, and promised earnestly to seek for strength to avoid temptation. A few weeks elapsed, and on my return, the answer to "Where is Brown?" was, "In the guard-house; he got better, got a pass, and, of course, came home drunk."

A severe illness followed; this occurred again and again; the necessity for air and exercise gained him occasionally a pass from the surgeons, always followed by the same sad result. The men despised him, treated him accordingly, and his case seemed hopeless. One day, one of our poor men, who was in a dying condition, fancied a piece of fresh shad —it was one of those sick longings, which, of course, we were anxious to gratify. Permission gained to send for it, I turned to one of the men at my side, and said, "Will you go to the market and get it for him?" Brown, who was standing near, sprang eagerly forward, "Oh! do let me go for you; I won't be a minute, and the doctor said a walk would be good for me." The sad doubt in my mind must have written itself upon my face, for its effect was reflected by the deep pain and wounded expression in his own. My resolution was taken instantly, and I resolved to risk it. Holding the money to him, I said, "Take it, then, and come back quickly." The blood rushed to his face, and the beaming look of gratitude made me sure that this was the best mode of treating him. Men are too often just what they are assumed to be; treat them as men of honor, such they will be; treat them as knaves, such also they will be. I mean not to affirm that there is no such thing as abstract truth or principle; far from it; but I do mean to say, that where the moral sense is weak, far more is gained by treating men as though we trusted, than as though we doubted. It is the unconscious tribute paid, all the world over, to honor and virtue. They would fain be or appear to be, all that we think them; and who can tell how far we may aid a sinking soul by the kind word of hopeful trust; or, on the other hand, by assuming a man to be utterly degraded, help to make him become so, in reality?

And yet, scarcely had Brown left my sight, ere the doubt returned. He had been doing better lately. I had thrown him into temptation; would he have strength to avoid it? Visions of illness, disgrace, suffering, and the guard-house, filled my mind. These thoughts were not dissipated by M.'s sudden question,

"Who did you send for that fish? How long he stays!"

With something of a pang of conscience, although quite aware that I had acted from the best motives, I said, courageously,

"I sent Brown; it is not so very long."

"Brown! Oh! how could you? You know what will happen?"

As I rely upon her judgment more than my own, my anxiety is not relieved, though concealed. The minutes grow to hours, and still no tidings of him. Another trial; the wardmaster appears.

"G—— wants to know if you've got his fish? you promised to send at once."

"Not yet," I said, "but I hope I shall very soon."

A very faint hope, it must be confessed. As he left the ladies' room, I heard one of the men say to him,

"G——'ll get no fish to-day. Do you know who she sent? Brown, if you'll believe it."

A prolonged whistle. "Didn't she know?"

"She might have, by this time, one would think.'"

Heart sick, I turned away; my theory of trust henceforth must have exceptions. I had led another into sin, and he must suffer for my fault. Just at this instant Brown rushes in, flushed and heated, it is true, but with exercise alone,— that was quite plain—and handing me the money, pants out,

"I've been clean to the wharf, and could'nt get a bit; I determined you should have it, and I've been through every market I knowed on, but not a blessed scrap could I find."

"How glad I am!" broke involuntarily from my lips; and I was only recalled to the inappropriateness of the reply, by his look of puzzled wonder, and "What was it you said, miss?"

"Nothing," I answered; "thank you for the trouble you have taken;" and he left me, much mystified by my evident delight at the failure of his errand.

The truth of his statement was verified by a lady, who (her carriage at the door) offered to see if she could be more successful. She returned, some time afterwards, bringing some other fish, and assuring me that it was quite impossible to procure any shad that day, at any price, as there was none in the market.

> " They tell me, that I should not love
>   Where I cannot esteem ;
>   But do not fear them, for to me
>   False wisdom doth it seem.

> " Nay,—rather I should love thee more
>   The farther thou dost rove ;
>   For what Prayers are effectual,
>   If not the Prayers of Love ? "

DARLINGTON.

"I PITY our sick men, to-day," thought I, as I gladly took shelter within the hospital walls from the burning summer sun, which was beating with unusual violence upon the hot brick pavements and dusty streets. The city in summer, and "Dante's Inferno," always seem to me synonymous terms. It is on days like these, when the town seems so close and crowded, the heated air so heavy and impure, that I long to have the hospitals or their occupants all moved to the calm, cool country, where the poor sufferer may be beguiled from the thought of his pain by the sweet sights and sounds ever around him; that blessed blue, which no town sky can ever attain, let it try its best, broken by fair, floating masses of white clouds, their forms ever varying, yet each seeming more beautiful than the last; the glad, grateful green of woods and dells, which, like a loved presence, ever unconsciously soothes and satisfies; the soft, springing wild flowers, with their sweet, sunny smile,—these for the eye; while for the ear, listen to the cheerful chime with which that little babbling brook plays its accompaniment in "little sharps and trebles"

to the chorus of voices overhead; no discord there
—not one false note to jar the unstrung nerve, but
all pure, perfect harmony.

Is there no medicine in all this? Rather, is it
not worth, for purposes of cure, all, and more than
all that the whole Materia Medica can offer? And
yet there are men living on this earth who tell
you, aye, even as though they were in earnest in
the assertion, too, that they do not love the country
—they prefer a city life. For such, I can only hope
that retributive justice may bestow upon them a
summer's campaign in one of our city hospitals.

"Have you seen our new lot of wounded?"

"No. When did they come in? Any serious
cases?"

"Only a few days ago. Yes, ma'am, some pretty
bad wounds; worse than we've had yet—two of
them can hardly live; but take care of one of
them, when you go in; he's as cross as thunder,
if you go within a mile of his bed."

This from one of the orderlies of the first ward,
as my hand was upon the latch of the door. I
confess the announcement was somewhat alarming,
as we could then be but a few rods from his bed;
however, "forewarned, forearmed." I enter, and
find the scene little different from usual, save that
the vacant beds are all filled, and a few more have
been added to the number, as they evidently stand
much closer than they do ordinarily. I pass on to

the familiar faces, and after a greeting with them, my attention is ˉattracted by a bright, cheerful tune, whistled in a voice of uncommon sweetness. It comes from that bed where that poor arm is bandaged from shoulder to finger tip, and, right glad am I to hear it; the men who are cheerful, are, as a rule, always the first to recover. He stops as I come up.

"I am glad you can whistle; it shows you are not suffering so much as I feared, when I saw your bandages."

He smiles, but says nothing; and I notice, as I come closer, that large drops of perspiration are standing in beads upon his brow; his one free hand is tightly clenched, and a nervous tremor runs over his whole frame.

One of my friends in a neighboring bed says, "Ah, Miss ——, you don't know Robinson yet, he's a new fellow, and we all laugh at him here; he says when the pain's just so bad he can't bear it nohow, he tries to whistle with all his might, and he finds it does him good."

Whether from the suspension of this novel remedy for acute suffering, or a sudden increase of pain, I cannot tell; but as I turn to Robinson for a confirmation of this singular statement, the large tears are in his eyes, and roll slowly down his cheeks. He tries to smile, however, and says, "Oh, yes! it does help me wonderfully; it kind

7 *

of makes me forget the pain, and think I'm at
home again, where I'm always whistling. Nothing
like keeping up a good heart. It don't always ache
like this—only in spells—it'll stop after a bit. Never
mind me, ma'am, I'm not half so bad as poor Darlington there."

There seemed to me something touching in the
extreme, in this earnest effort to subdue suffering
by whistling up the bright memories of home, in
the midst of such intense physical anguish, and in
the endeavor to treat his own case as lightly as
possible. Well has it been said, " Character is seen
through small openings;" and as he appeared in
this conversation, such did we find him always.
Gentle, unselfish, and bearing his terrible suffering
with a beautiful patience, ere long he became a
general favorite throughout the whole hospital;
and during the tedious months of close and constant nursing which his case required, every one
seemed glad to help him and wait upon him at all
times. But this is anticipating, for no doubt he
will appear again, as for a long time he was one
of our prime objects of interest, from the constant
attention as to diet and delicacies which his case
required.

As I pass on from bed to bed, I give rather a
scrutinizing glance, in hopes of just seeing the
formidable object whom I had been warned to
avoid. But in vain. All seem quiet, and since my

presence has stopped the whistling, nothing is heard but the men talking in an undertone, or an occasional low moan of pain, which seems to come from some one asleep and suffering. Suddenly, in my tour, I pause before a bed, struck by the expression of intense anguish on a sweet, young face, white as the pillow it rests upon; his fair hair tossed from the pale brow, which is painfully contracted, and his long, thin, taper fingers, white as the face, move convulsively as he sleeps. He is evidently badly wounded, for a hoop raises the clothes from his bandaged limb. Who can he be? Evidently those hands, even allowing for illness and loss of blood, have never seen rough service, and belong to some one of a higher class than we usually see as a Private here; for although we proudly acknowledge that some of the best blood of the country is now in the ranks, still it has not, as yet, been our good fortune to encounter its presence in this hospital. There is a sort of fascination about that face, and I stand gazing at him and wondering over him till Richards, one of our old attachés, comes up.

"Oh! he's asleep, poor fellow, at last; that accounts for it; the boys are all wondering how you got so close; he's in a great way, when he's awake. He couldn't bear you that near without screaming."

"Surely this can't be the man Foster said was 'as cross as thunder?'" said I, thinking it utterly

impossible that here was indeed the dreaded object
I had been seeking.

"Well, yes, miss; the boys call him cross, but
somehow I don't think he means to be cross; only,
you see he suffers so with that mashed-up limb,
that he's afraid they'll touch him when they come
near, and he calls out sudden like, and so they call
him cross; but he's as grateful as can be, for any
little thing you do for him."

"Is he very badly wounded?"

"Oh! yes. The doctors would have taken his
leg right off, but they say he's too weak to stand
it; you never saw such a sight; he and Robinson,
there, are an awful pair to look at."

"Is this Darlington? I heard Robinson say that
Darlington was worse than he was."

"Yes, ma'am; the doctor says he's not worse,
only they take it different. You see, poor Tom
here, frets all the time, and don't give himself no
chance; but that fellow over there'll worry through
yet, if pluck can do it."

This was afterwards confirmed by the surgeon
himself. He assured me that Robinson's wound
had appeared quite as dangerous — indeed, at one
time, even more so; but his quiet, placid disposition
aided his recovery immensely; while the terribly
nervous temperament, and high state of nervous
irritability of poor Darlington, were equally against
him.

"I'm glad enough he's sleeping," added Richards, "for he's been here for three days, and this is the first time, night or day, that I've caught him with his eyes shut; lots of anodyne, too, the doctors give him. It's worry, worry, worry from morning to night about his sister; he wants so to see her, and says if she were only here, she could come near his bed and it wouldn't hurt him."

"Where does she live? Why don't they send for her? he can't live."

"Away off in Michigan; and he won't even have her told that he's sick; he says wait till he's better, and then he'll write; but he won't have her frightened. If he could only forget her for a little while, it's my notion he'd do better; but I tell him none of the boys here make half the fuss after their wives that he does after his sister. Poor boy! he's just twenty-one since he came in here, and I rather guess they must have thought a sight of him at home,—at least, he does of them,—too much for his own good, that's certain; this terrible fretting after home, when they're sick, does the boys a lot of harm."

Knowing that Richards' one talent was garrulity, I left him and went to our room, thinking that perhaps we might prepare something to tempt poor Darlington's appetite; for the surgeon told us it was vital to keep up his strength, and yet he

could scarcely be persuaded to touch anything
which had been brought him.

As I well knew, from the state they described
him to be in, that the sight of a stranger could
not be agreeable to him, we sent everything we
made for him through Richards, who constituted
himself his body-guard from the moment of his
entering the hospital, and a most faithful and
untiring nurse he proved. Never again can I say
that garrulity is his only talent; he developed then
and there a gift for nursing for which those who
best loved Darlington can never be too grateful.
Days passed on, and I soon found that (as I had
supposed) what the men termed " crossness," was
but the sad querulousness produced by suffering,
and the state of which I have spoken.

While Robinson evidently gained,—though his
attacks of pain were still marked by his own
peculiar whistling, which we constantly heard in
the ladies' room, and always knew how to interpret,
—Darlington was as evidently losing; and all hopes
of amputation were necessarily abandoned. I could
feel nothing but the most intense pity for him, and
longing to comfort him; but it seemed impossible.
M. said to me one day, " It certainly seems best,
from what we see and hear of Darlington. to send,
not take, his nourishment to him; and yet, perhaps
our presence might be more welcome; but I hesitate,

because the sight of any one coming near him seems to throw him into such a nervous state."

"Yes," said I, "any one but Richards; doesn't it seem a strange fancy?"

And so we went on, for a week or more longer; for our interest in the case was so great, that even when not on duty at the hospital, we felt that we must know its progress. One day the surgeon came to me and begged me to try to cheer up Darlington, he was so down-hearted, would taste no food, etc.; must certainly sink unless some change could be made in his feelings. I went to his bedside at once, to see if he were awake, for much of the time he was kept under the effect of anodyne, to deaden the excessive pain. For many a long day did that look of deep, profound wretchedness haunt me, as he raised his soft, clear blue eyes to mine, and said, in the most earnest, pleading tone, "Dear lady, please to go away, I am so very wretched." Any one who had ever suffered realized that there was no crossness here; physical suffering, acute and intense, was written in every line of his face, sounded in every tone of his voice, and most earnestly did I long to soothe him.

Without answering, I drew back, and laid my cold hands on his burning brow. His whole expression changed. "You like it," I said; "I am so glad; we have all been wishing so much to do something to comfort you."

A sweet smile, more touching than tears, passed over the poor white face, followed the next moment by the painful contraction of the muscles from suffering.

"But I want *her!*"

"Ah!" said I, "that sister! No one can take her place; we will write, and she can soon be here; she would come further than from Michigan, I am sure, to see a sick brother who loves her as you do."

With more energy than I had ever seen in him, he lifted his head from the pillow, saying eagerly, "Never, never write to her; I wouldn't have her see me so for all——"

But here, either from the effort, or from a sudden increase of pain, faintness came on; strong stimulants and the doctor's presence were needed, and I left him. This, I trusted, however, might be a beginning.

The next day, when I came to him, he looked much sunken, and seemed altogether lower than I had yet seen him. He smiled, however, and tried to lift his hand, and point to his head.

"You like my cold hands," said I, as I once more pressed them on his throbbing temples; "but perhaps this hot day, a little ice would be better; let me get you some."

He said something which I could not catch; his voice sounded strangely weak and broken, and I was obliged to ask him to repeat it.

"No! oh no! I said your hands were better than any ice."

"They put you in mind of that sister, is that it? Well, shut your eyes now, and try to fancy, just for a little while, that they are really hers, and that she is standing in my place, where I know she would so long to be."

"That sister," he said, quietly and gently, "whom I shall never see on this earth again."

This was the first time that he had so spoken; always before he had alluded to being better—to getting home—to writing himself to her; but now it seemed he felt and realized his state.

These were the last words I ever heard poor Darlington speak, for I never saw him again. My week at the hospital was over; I was obliged to leave home for a short time, and when I returned he was at peace, and calmly laid to rest.

> "Out of the darkness, into the light:
> No more sickness, no more sighing;
> No more suffering, self-denying;
> No more weakness, no more pain;
> Never a weary soul again;
> No more clouds, and no more night;—
> Out of the darkness into the light."

Although I was not present, I had the most touching account of his last hours from one who,

8

in truth, acted a sister's part,—watched by him, comforted, consoled, pointed him upward, and received his latest breath. With her own hands she cut off a lock of that fair hair for the poor sister, so fondly and so truly loved in her far-away home.

She told me, in speaking of the last days of his life, that after I had left, and as death drew near, all that restlessness and irritability passed away, and that he lay calm and peaceful as a little child; talked to her quietly — sent messages to his home — gave particular directions as to his funeral — saying that it would satisfy them all at home, to know everything had been carefully attended to, and that they would see that it was all paid for. Every wish was carried out; his body was wrapped in the Flag; our own grand Service for the Dead said over him; his faithful nurse, "Uncle Richards," following him to his grave,— in one of the lots generously given by one of the cemeteries in the neighborhood of the city. It was a great comfort to know that he looked at Death without fear; his mind had evidently been dwelling much and deeply upon the subject, during many of those long hours when we had supposed him to be in a stupor. He expressed a sure and steadfast trust in the merits of his dear Lord and Saviour, and rested with a quiet confidence upon His mercy. He passed away calmly and gently, and we have perfect trust that he sleeps in Paradise. Such was the account I received on my return.

> "And, comforted, I praised the grace
> Which him had led to be
> An early seeker of That Face
> Which he should early see."

Perhaps the most pathetic part of the whole thing, was to see the deep, real, unostentatious grief of poor Richards, who seemed as if he had lost a son. This was a strange case altogether. Richards was a man who had been in the English army; tall, fine-looking, with a military air and bearing, which had impressed me much when he first came to the hospital; but I soon found that his habits were bad, and that any permission to go out was sure to be followed by a night in the guard-house, and days in bed. And yet a kinder heart could scarcely be found. He had devoted himself to more than one of the men, and watched them night after night till their death. In one instance, when one man whom he had been nursing was to be taken home, here in the city, he obtained permission to go with him and nurse him, sitting up with him and watching him till his death. As at such times he always remained perfectly sober, it was suggested to make him nurse, (his disease rendering a return to his regiment impossible,) with the hope that the good influence over him which this work seemed to possess, might be permanent;

but this would not do; he could not be trusted unless he had a special interest in the man he was nursing, and what was necessary to create such interest he alone knew. Whatever the qualities were, Darlington possessed them in the highest degree. He seemed to attract him from the first, and the love was warmly returned. Darlington thought no one could move him, no one could feed him, no one could dress his wound but " Uncle Richards, dear Uncle Richards," as he called him; and often have I wondered at the tender love which seemed to exist between them. Those who were present told me that it was truly wonderful to watch Richards all through that last day, kneeling at his bedside, praying with him, repeating text after text of Scripture or hymns, as he asked for them. One of the last things Darlington said was, " Where is dear Uncle Richards? I want to put my arms round his neck, and thank him for all his goodness and kindness to me."

And yet this is the man of whom some one said to me, only a day or two since, " Why do you speak to that worthless fellow?"

One day, in my next week at the hospital, Richards came to me, and with the usual salute, which he never forgets, said, " Miss ——, you used to care for poor Tom, would you let me tell you about him? The world seems so lonely to me, now he's gone."

I gladly assented, and seated on an old packing-box, in the corner of the hospital entry, I listened to his story. He gave me every detail of his illness, most of them already familiar to me; told, with evident pride, how the poor fellow thought nobody but himself could do anything for him.

"You mind, miss, don't you, how the first day you saw him, I told you he didn't mean to be cross, though the boys thought him so? Well, he told me before he died, how sorry he was they had thought so, but they could never know what agony it was to him to see them come near him; but now he felt that he ought to have tried to bear it all more patiently. Poor Tom! there's not been many like him here, and there'll never be any like him to me," and hard, heavy sobs shook his whole frame.

I spoke to him of the comfort he had been to him; of the kind way in which he had watched him, and how we had all noticed it; and won a promise from him, in his softened state, that henceforward he would try so to live as to meet him hereafter; and I really believe that at the time he was sincere; but habit is a fearful thing, and the struggle against a sin so confirmed more fearful still.

Some days afterwards, he came to me, when there were others present, and said:

"I had a letter from *her* to-day."

8*

My thoughts were far enough from Darlington at the moment, and I answered,

"From whom?"

"From *her*, you know!"

"And who do you mean by 'her?'"

"His sister, to be sure," he said, in an injured tone, as though I should have known that, at present, there was but one subject for him.

"Oh, have you? What does she say?"

"Not now, not now," he said, looking at the others, as though the grief were too fresh, the subject too sacred, to be mentioned so publicly; "but I just thought you'd like to know."

At a quiet moment, the next day, he begged me to let him tell me what she had written;—her warm, earnest thanks to him for all his love and tenderness to her darling brother; and begging him to plant some flowers where he was laid to rest. This may never be in his power, but there are those who will never forget to care for and cherish the low grave of that young Private.

MILITARY HOSPITAL, July, 1862.

> What matters it, one more, or less?
>   A Private died to-day;
> "Bring up a stretcher—bear him off—
>   And take that bed away;
> Put 39 into his place,
>   It is more airy there;
> And give his knapsack, and those clothes,
>   Into the steward's care."

So, it is over.   All is done!
    And, ere the evening guard,
Few thought of the Dread Presence
    That day within the ward.—
Few thought of the young Private,
    Whose suffering, pallid brow
Was knit by torture, not by time,—
    Unfurrow'd by Life's plough.

Few thought upon the agony
    In that far western home,
Where he, their hearts' best treasure,
    Was never more to come;
For Privates have both hearts and homes,
    And Privates, too, can love;
And Privates' prayers, thank God for that!
    May reach the Throne above.

We know thee not, sad sister!
    Whose name so oft he breathed,
Till it would seem that thoughts of thee
    Round his whole being wreathed;
But by the love he bore for thee,
    We catch a glimpse of thine;
And, by the bond of sisterhood,
    We meet beside his shrine.

We meet to tell thee, stricken soul!
    That strangers held thy place—
Sisters by Nature's right, and he,
    Brother, by right of race.
While pillow'd tenderly his head,
    Cooled was his burning brain
By loving hands; and one fair curl,
    Severed for thee, sweet pain!

If comfort be not mockery
    In such a harrowing hour,
O, find it in his cherishing,
    And let the thought have power;
Thy brain must turn, or so thou deem'st,
    He, needing love and care,
Knowing 'twas granted, thou canst kneel
    And ask for strength to bear.

O men, his brothers, bear in mind,
　For all, our dear Lord died!
Souls own but one Commission—
　Love of The Crucified!
Right gallant are the Officers—
　Men, noble, brave, and true;
But when you breathe a Prayer for them,
　Say one for Privates too.

"LITTLE CORNING."

LET no one imagine that hospital life is all gloom. Sickness and suffering are, of course, the normal condition, but we try to crowd in all the brightness we can; games, gayety, and gladness, have their place. One such presence as that of " Little Corning" must insure some sunshine. How can I describe that quaint, droll, merry little sergeant, once seen, never to be forgotten?

" Little Corning," we always called him, to distinguish him from our tall wardmaster of the same name; and most appropriate, too, did it seem to his little, short, squat figure. I always contended that he had been a sailor, from the roll and pitch in his gait, and a certain way he had of giving a lurch whenever he wanted to reach anything near him. He assured me most positively that such was not the case; but I still continue to think that he must have been, in some former state of existence, if not in this. Many men have been convicted before now on circumstantial evidence, why should not he be also? Perhaps he did not choose to confess the fact — no man is bound to criminate himself — therefore I see no good reason for giving up my first conviction, and many for holding it; ergo, I repeat that I think he had been a sailor.

I never heard a merrier laugh, or knew a happier nature. He seemed to possess the blessed faculty of shedding sunshine and joy all around him; many a harsh word has been hushed, many an incipient quarrel checked, by his odd, dry way of placing things in a ludicrous light, and thus changing churlishness into cheerfulness, moroseness into merriment. Momus certainly presided at his birth, touched him with his wand, and claimed him for his own.

He had the best reason for his uniform cheerfulness; indeed, the only one which can ever secure it. His Christianity was of a truly healthy order, and certainly brought him both content and peace. During his residence of many months in the hospital, I never saw a frown upon his face, or heard anything but a bright, joyous laugh, or pleasant word from him. Often, in my rounds, I would come upon him, unexpectedly, in some obscure corner, poring over his Bible, apparently quite absorbed in it, and yet always ready to lay it aside when he could make himself useful, but returning to it as a pleasure, when his work was accomplished.

He had a remarkably fine tenor voice, and I have often seen men of all sorts and tastes gathered round him, listening by the hour to Methodist hymns, for the sake, we must suppose, of those uncommon tones, rather than of the words which called them forth.

One morning he came into the ladies' room, and informed us, with much delight, that Mr. —— had promised to ask some of the pupils from the Blind Asylum to come to the hospital the next evening, to give a concert, begging us to be present.

I told him that, for one of us, that would be quite impossible; it would be pleasant, but could not be arranged. He seemed much disappointed, but soon left the room, and I had forgotten all about it, when, an hour or two later, he burst into the room, quite radiant, exclaiming, " It's all fixed, we've got it all fixed."

" What's all fixed?" said I, my mind intent on some refractory oysters which refused to boil.

" The concert, to be sure. Mr. —— has arranged it for to-morrow afternoon, and now you'll come."

I thanked him, and gladly accepted for us both, promising to make all our necessary preparations for the supper of our sick men, quite early, so that we might be ready in time. At the appointed hour, the next afternoon, " Little Corning " presented himself.

" Come, ladies, come quickly ! the boys are all in the dining-room; I've brought chairs for you, and they're quite ready to begin."

"Wait a minute; not just yet; sick men come first."

"Oh! please now, come, won't you? Suppose just for once that the boys are sick on the field, and never mind them to-night."

"For shame, sergeant! Such counsel from you? We cannot believe it. Go in, and we will follow you."

But although music is his passion, and he is burning to be there, he gallantly prefers to wait, and be our escort; and in pity for him, we hurry as much as possible; and now we are done; let us go.

There are our chairs, all arranged for us. What a crowd! At least, a crowd for our number of well men,—over a hundred, certainly; all who are fit to be out of their beds, and some who, we very well know, are not. See how they are jammed together; on benches, on the dining-table itself, in the windows, and on every available spot, battered and bandaged, *wrappered* and wrinkled, suffering and smiling, in one promiscuous mass. Look at that pale boy, sitting on the corner of the table on our right; he has been as ill as possible with typhoid fever, and surely can never sit through the concert in that position. Let him try for a while, however; the whole scene will do him more good, by amusing and diverting his mind, than the exertion can do him harm. Truly, as we glance around, it is a strange scene. Men from North, East, and West, gathered together — in dress and undress uniform; from the cavalry jacket, with its yellow facings, to dressing-gowns and even shirt-sleeves; all eagerly and earnestly bent upon one idea; but even as they gaze, can you not read their characters, and place their homes? Each State has its own characteristics so strongly marked, that I have often laughingly promised to tell each man in a ward, from whence he came; and after a little practice, one seldom makes a mistake, — at least never wanders far from the truth; but we cannot stop to discuss that point now, as the songs are beginning.

But stop! It cannot be. Look, M., look! It actually is. Our naughty, disobedient, handsome Harry, with his bandaged limb on a chair, over there by the window. Only this morning did I hear the surgeon give orders to have that limb put in a fracture-trough, as the only means to preserve perfect stillness for it. I saw, later, that it had been done; and now look — everything removed, and here he is. That was a very severe wound, from which he has been suffering for many months; he told me yesterday, that, in all, fifty pieces of bone had been taken out of his leg; the surgeons rather pride themselves on having prevented the necessity of amputation by the closest watching and care; and we cannot help feeling

provoked with him for persisting in moving about,
when perfect rest is so essential to his cure.   And
yet, who could ever be angry with Harry, for any
length of time?   He has a way of his own of winning us over to his side, and we know what a warm
heart beats beneath that wilfulness; but arguments
with him are of little avail; the other day, in reply
to my earnest remonstrances, he said :

"But, Miss ——, my leg is my own, and if I like
to have a little fun now, and lose it afterwards, will
any one but myself suffer ?"

We have almost given him up as incorrigible.
Patriotic songs are fast following each other,—and
certainly the applause is "sui generis."   Crutches
pounded on the floor, and splints hammered on the
table, with an energy and fervor which threaten
their own destruction; but the sightless singers
receive it all apparently with the greatest satisfaction, deeming that the greater the noise, the
greater the pleasure, and probably such is the
case.

Listen.   What is that tall singer saying?   He
has already twice repeated it, but he cannot hope
to be heard in this confusion.   See !—he is trying
again : "I want you all to be quite still now, and
listen to this song; make no noise, if you please."

An instant hush, and eager expectation on every
face. The singer begins the well-known " Laughing

Chorus,"—well-known here, but evidently a perfect novelty to these listeners.

For a few moments there is an effort to maintain quiet, but suddenly their pent-up feelings break forth, and peal after peal of heartiest laughter rings through the room. In vain they try to stop —a moment's pause, and the singer's voice is heard, seeming only to give the key-note, which one after another takes up, till, in the wild storm that follows, they are entirely unaware that he has come to a conclusion — that it is all over and done, and the singers are leaving. Just at this moment my eye is caught by our friend, the sergeant, his head resting on the table, his face almost purple, and his whole frame literally convulsed with laughter.

"Corning! Corning! stop! you will be sick."

But in vain; that laugh must be laughed out; and he cannot even recover himself sufficiently to join in the vote of thanks which the men are offering to the kind friend who had given them this enjoyment.

The next morning, when I arrived, I said to M. at once, "How is Harry, to-day?"

"Not in the least the worse, by his own account; but I hear Little Corning is in bed—actually made sick, from the effects of the concert."

This scarcely surprised me, as I had feared it, knowing that he was far from strong.

A little later in the morning, something called

me over to the ward in which he was, and as I
entered I heard a groan; to my surprise, it came
from our little friend, who was, as M. had heard, in
bed, and evidently suffering.

"Why, sergeant," said I, "I am sorry to see that
the concert has had such a bad effect."

But at my approach the groan was turned into
a hearty laugh, though it was quite plain that the
suffering continued.

"Oh! Miss ——, don't, please don't! I can't
begin again. I ache all over in each separate
muscle, and I've lost all faith in you."

"I don't want you to begin again; but what do
you mean by having 'lost faith in me?'"

"Why, don't you remember, you always said a
good laugh was the best medicine?—and it's come
near killing me—oh, dear! oh, dear!"

"That bottle, standing on the table at your side,
Corning, is marked to be taken by the teaspoonful;
perhaps, if you were to empty it at a dose, it might
have the same effect. I never recommended such
immoderate laughter."

"Oh, please don't speak of it. It brings it up
so."

The remembrance was quite too much, and one
fit of laughter followed another, strangely inter-
spersed with groans of pain, from the soreness of
the muscles. That merry laugh was at all times
most contagious; the men quickly crowded round,

joining in it without asking any reason, and we bade fair to have the scene of yesterday re-enacted.

To preserve gravity was quite impossible, there was something so irresistibly ludicrous in the whole affair, but I felt that it must be stopped.

"Corning! this will never do; you must control yourself; you will be ill; and besides, you are disturbing our sick men."

"I think, Miss ——," said he, with a violent effort at composure, "if you won't take it hard, if you'd just go away; if I didn't see you, I might get quiet."

"Certainly I will. I won't 'take it hard,' at all, and I will come back when you are quieter."

"Oh! please no! Oh! don't come back; if you do, it'll be as bad as ever again."

The idea was quite enough; and the last sound I heard, as I withdrew my mirth-inspiring presence, was another of those clear, ringing laughs. How I longed to have the same effect upon the poor fellows in another ward, where I had vainly racked my brain for many days, to call up even a faint smile on their depressed and weary faces. I sent everything over to the sergeant's ward through the day, not risking my dangerous presence there; and even at night judged it better not to go over to say goodbye, although it was Saturday night, and my duties for the week were over.

When I came again, my merry friend had been

9 *

returned to his regiment, and that had been our
final interview. I have often wondered since, how
(if ever) we should meet again? Whether that
last laughing parting will linger in his mind, or
whether its memory shall have been crushed out
by the stern realities of war?

NOTE.—The problem has been solved. To our amazement, the
week after the Gettysburg fight, Little Corning walked into the
ladies' room at the hospital, fresh from the field—or rather, anything
but fresh. Tattered and battered, soiled and moiled; his head tied
up, and looking very much, on the whole, as though he had been in
an Irish row. He had been wounded in the temple by a shell; but
not dangerously, and had hastened to "his old home," as he called
it, as soon as he arrived, although to his great regret, as well as ours,
he had been placed in another hospital.

We welcomed him warmly, and were too full of his danger and
our own — his escape and our own, to revert to past days for more
than a word. He had not lost his old bright spirit, and when we told
him how pleasant it was to have our old friends for our defenders, his
eye sparkled, and he said, "Yes; I felt all the time I was fighting
for you." And thus we met again.

"No stream from its source
Flows seaward, how lonely soever its course,
But what some land is gladdened. No star ever rose
And set, without influence somewhere. Who knows
What earth needs from earth's lowest creature? No life
Can be pure in its purpose, and strong in its strife,
And all life not be purer and stronger thereby:
The spirits of just men made perfect on high;
The Army of Martyrs who stand by the throne,
And gaze into The Face that makes glorious their own,
Know this surely at last. Honest love, honest sorrow;
Honest work for the day, honest hope for the morrow,—
Are these worth nothing more than the hand they make weary?
The heart they have saddened, the life they leave dreary?
Hush! the sevenfold Heavens to the voice of the Spirit
Echo, 'He that o'ercometh, shall all things inherit.'"

GAVIN.

How sadly and how strangely we misjudge our brother! We walk daily by his side, and receive the cold exterior as a type of the inner life, forgetting that hardness, sternness, and repelling reserve, may be only the crust of the crater, hiding the lava beneath. How comes it that, when, in our own case, we are all so well aware that,

"Not ev'n the tenderest heart, and next, our own,
Knows half the reasons why we smile or sigh;"

yet, we will not believe in the secret sufferings of others? Instead of seeking to win the unstrung instrument back to harmony, by the tender touch of loving sympathy, we mete out precisely the measure meted to us; oppose coldness to coldness, hardness to hardness, reserve to reserve, and thus a wall is built up between us, and all hope of influence is gone. We need more trust in, and more charity for, each other. Woe to the sick soul, suffering and sorrowful, its sickness only shown by the petulant word, the rude retort, the outward expression of inward wretchedness,—woe to such a soul, I say, were it left only to man's tender mercies. Most mercifully it is not. Infinite Love breathes balm upon it. Infinite Compassion soothes it. When shall we even begin to imitate the one, or strive to attain to the other?

These thoughts were called up by a keen sense of the injustice of my own judgment, in a special case, only discovered this very day.

A sunny, bright afternoon. Our men are all improving, none dangerously ill; the most of them have sought the yard, to walk, to smoke, to sing, or play at such games as cannot be carried on in-doors. Everything has a more cheerful aspect than usual. If melancholy and depression are infectious, so, happily, are mirth and gayety; and as the chorus of one of our favorite army songs rings out on the air, I find myself joining in it, as I spring up the stairs, two at a time, on an errand. Scarcely noticing where I am going, I suddenly stumble upon something on the stair.

"Why, Gavin, can that be you?"

Dashed upon the floor, his face buried in his hands, his whole attitude denoting utter despair, he does not even move or notice my question.

While I am standing, looking and wondering, let me give you a little knowledge of him, as he appears in the wards. Some time since I was much struck, on coming to the hospital, by the soldier acting as guard at the door. His erect and military bearing, well-made figure, and broad chest, with the certain "je ne sais quoi" of a gentleman,

rather impressed me, as he lifted his cap and
saluted as I approached.

"Who is our gentlemanly guard to-day?" said I
to M., on entering our room.

"Just come; a fine-looking fellow, isn't he? I
have just been finding out his history. He is terribly reserved, but I have made out that he is a
Northerner who went to the South to settle; was
impressed, sorely against his will, at the time of
the breaking out of the war; was taken ill, and
allowed, as he was useless, to come here to see his
mother, who was also ill; he, of course, never
returned, although he had letters from his Colonel,
which he showed, first offering him a Lieutenancy,
and then a Captaincy; but he prefers, he says, to
be a Private in our own army, to the highest
position in theirs."

"Well?" said I, as she paused.

"That's all; he told me nothing more; but that
as soon as he came North he enlisted, was taken
sick in camp, and sent here."

"His history, then, is still to hear," I said; "he
hasn't accounted for his interesting melancholy, or
the mournful expression of those large, dark eyes,
which strike you the moment you look at him;
and yet there is something about him—a sort of
dark look—which I don't altogether fancy."

"Oh! you want to make up a romantic story for
him, do you? Well, find it out, if you can; I have

told you all that he would tell me, and yet, I confess I was struck with his language; it was certainly
much above that of most of our men here."

Weeks passed by, and as Gavin was not sick
enough to need care, we had little to do with him,
and that little did not encourage us to go further.
Often a word of greeting, in passing, will call forth
something more, but his cold, forbidding manner,
joined to a certain distant politeness, so repelled
me, that I resolved to let him alone; and yet I
felt sorry for him, for I could not fail to notice his
unpopularity among the men. He walked alone,
mentally and physically, and seemed to desire no
intercourse with any one.

One morning I found him gloomily seated in a
corner of the ward, apparently unconscious of
everything around him.

"What a terribly long face," said I, trying to
rally him; "you will never get well till you learn
to laugh."

"To laugh!" said he, with intense bitterness;
"then I am invalided for life. Little enough is
there on earth to laugh about, I think;" and rising
hastily, he brushed past me, and left the ward.

"I don't like that Gavin," I said to M., "there's
something so dark and hard about him; I can't
make him out."

"Ah! no story yet? I thought he was to have
a romantic story, with his interesting dark eyes."

"Story! He never opens his lips to any one; and unless he shall need something, I have almost determined never to open mine to him again."

Such was the man whom I have left all this time lying upon the staircase. Knowing as I did that whatever his faults might be, intemperance was not one of them, I once more address him; he evidently has not heard me before, for, starting up hastily, and forgetting his usual politeness, he exclaims, petulantly, " I thought I could be to myself here, at least."

"So you can, as far as I am concerned; I merely came up stairs on an errand, without an idea that you were here; but another time when you wish to secure perfect privacy, I should scarcely advise you to choose a staircase."

"It matters little," said he, sitting down on the stairs, resting his elbows on his knees. and burying his face in his hands, "one part of the world or another; it's all the same; dark enough to wish to be well out of it."

" Gavin," said I, sitting down on the stair beside him, "do you remember that you told me how terribly your back ached from carrying your knapsack and blanket on that long march ?"

A dull, uninterested assent.

" What would have been most welcome, when the pain became intolerable?"

10

"To unload, of course;" his head still buried in his hands.

"At times, in the long march of life, I have borne a heavy, moral knapsack; and when the pain from its weight became intolerable, no words can tell the relief of unloading, and sharing the burden with some loving heart, with whom it was as safe and as sacred as with myself. Your heart, just now, is aching worse than ever did your back; might it not ease it to try the experiment?"

He raised his head quickly; fire enough in those eyes then.

"Ease it!" he said; "doesn't it feel every day and every hour that it must burst, unless I tell what I am suffering? I walk among the men here, and they pass me as cold and stiff, when, God knows, I'm on fire inside; I'm burning up, burning up, here," added he, pressing his hand on his brain.

This was enough. The buckles were unstrapped, the burden would follow.

The first thing that roused us was the tap of the drum for supper. The long hours of that sunny summer's afternoon had slipped by, as I listened to a story, which, in Victor Hugo's hands, would be worked into a romance quite as thrilling as anything he has ever penned; whilst in mine it must remain forever,—a deposit sacred as the grave. My object was accomplished. With a

smile, he rose — the first I had ever seen on his
face—saying, "You were right about that moral
knapsack; my heart feels lighter than I ever
thought it could again."

"And you will do as I say?"

"I will try."

"And you will try too, won't you, to remember
my first advice, some time since, and learn to laugh
a little more?"

"Indeed I will; and it seems as if it might be
possible now, but let me tell you——"

"Nothing more to-day," said I, laughing; "I
must refuse any further confidence;" and running
down stairs to our room, I was complimented upon
the promptitude with which I performed an errand.
No matter, thought I;—if one sad soul has found
comfort in pouring out the bitter sorrows of a life,
the hours have not rolled by in vain. Are we not
all responsible for each day, nay, for each hour, as
it passes? Not alone for the right use of time in
improving our own souls, but for the manner in
which we act upon others. Influence! The language scarcely holds a more solemn word,— the
mind scarcely receives a more fearful thought!
How has this power been exerted? We all possess
it in greater or less degree. We all shall have to
render an account for the use or misuse of such a
terrible talent.

> "The deeds we do, the words we say,
> Into still air they seem to fleet;
> We count them ever past,
> But they shall last;—
> In the dread judgment, they
> And we shall meet!"

Time was, when, to my mind, it seemed only humility to believe that such a speck in God's creation — such an atom, great in no one thing, mentally, morally, or physically—must be without power for good or evil — without influence upon any single soul. It will not do. Humility is doubtless a great gift; Truth is a greater. No mortal being into whom God has breathed the breath of life, can live upon this earth and not act upon his fellow mortals in some manner. We cannot be merely negative; we are, we must be positive.

> "Where we disavow
> Being keeper to our brother, we're his Cain."

A word, a look, aye, even a tone may be the making or undoing of a soul. My brother! remember that to those amongst whom you are thrown, you must be, morally, either air or water. Air, to fan the smouldering spark of good, till its white flame mounts higher and higher, encircling your head with a halo of glory; or water, to quench that same spark, which, in dying, will envelop you in the blackness of darkness for ever and ever.

HASTY JUDGMENT.

How little, in this world of ours,
    One heart doth know another;
Man treads alone the path of life,
    A stranger to his brother.

The heart hath its own depths—it strives
    With sacred awe to hide,
E'en from those round us, journeying on
    Unconscious at our side.

Recesses, which, to the world's gaze,
    Are dark and barred from view;
Hence comes it that the public eye
    So rarely reads us true.

And yet a light does reach those depths—
    Those Portals have a key;
They're brightened by Love's silver beams,
    Unlocked by Sympathy.

Those ashes, which, to common view,
    Cold, dark, and lifeless seem,
When stirr'd by Sympathy's soft touch,
    Send forth a brilliant gleam.

Then pause, nor judge thy fellow man;
    Remember it may be,
The heart is beating underneath,
    But thou dost lack the key.

10 *

CHRISTMAS AT THE U. S. A. HOSPITAL, —— ——.

I PROMISED, when we parted, dear C., that you should have some account of our Christmas doings; but the busy days have slipped by, till now, without my finding a moment to redeem that promise.

You know how we are all occupied at that time; but no matter how much there is to be done, in these days "private interests" have a different signification, and demand attention.

The morning of Christmas Eve, therefore, found —— and myself on our way to the hospital. With that ready interest which, with her, always rises to meet the emergency, even at the busiest moments, she has offered to go with me and help us in our work; and you know how it doubles my pleasure for her to do so. Several of the ladies have agreed to meet here to-day; some for the purpose of superintending the cooking for the Christmas dinner, plum-puddings, etc.; others to make and put up the greens for the Christmas decoration; we, as you may suppose, are among the latter class. Our quiet ladies' room is quite a scene of bustle this morning; the ladies in charge for the week carry-

ing on, or attempting to carry on, their usual
duties; others flying in and out for various purposes; green wreaths strewing the floor, and vain
attempts are being made to twist them into some
available shape.

This confusion will never do. Nothing can be
accomplished in this way. Let us go into one of
the wards, where it is quiet; and soon we find
ourselves seated by the stove, endeavoring to form
a green sentence by covering the letters with moss
and ground pine; they have been nicely cut for us
by the genius of the hospital, and we are pressing
into our service all the men who can sew, or rather,
all who say that they can, which is sometimes quite
a different affair.

But before we begin, we must go and speak to
poor James, who has been so ill; he is actually
sitting up; but how pale and weak he looks, and
what a languid expression, as he smiles! He tells
us that he hopes to be in the dining-room to-morrow,
and in a few days to start for home. Ah! James,
that photograph so carefully concealed beneath
your pillow, peeps out occasionally, and we all
know that you left a two weeks' bride to serve
your country.

He has been suffering from fever; but worse
than this, he is subject to epileptic fits, which he
had hoped were cured; but hard life and exposure
have brought them back, and he has had several

very severe attacks since he has been here. His gentle, winning manner has made him a general favorite, and we are all glad to see him better. He begs to have his chair moved up to our circle, where he can, at least, look on, while we work; and he is always sure to find plenty of ready and willing hands to do any service that he needs.

But our work must not stand still; and lo! at this crisis, we find ourselves without implements. We had supposed we were simply to twine and festoon wreaths, instead of which, or rather, in addition, we find the green must be sewed on to those thick book-binders' board letters. Oh! why were they not pasteboard, and why have we no thimbles? But these are not the first wounds we have received in the service of our country; so, as we have a few needles, never mind, let us do our best; and, as our number is increasing,—one after another coming up "to see the fun," and being at once enlisted in our service,— no doubt we shall accomplish the task.

The men, who are always ready to help us, are specially so to-day, when the bright spirit of the season seems to communicate itself to all.

Is there not something singularly striking in thus preparing to hail the birth of the Prince of Peace in the midst of an army hospital, where we are surrounded by all the dreadful effects of war? Surely in no other spot. save the field of battle

itself, could we as fully appreciate the priceless
blessings contained in that Title.

Those who cannot sew, aid us in other ways.
One of our lieutenants prefers to collect the little
bunches of green, and hand them to me to sew on,
rather than try his hand at sewing himself; as he
is busily engaged at this work, one of the men, in
passing, laughingly rallies him on his occupation.

"Pretty work for a commissioned officer!"

"To oblige a lady, Horstman, is never beneath
any officer, no matter what his rank. General ——
himself will tell you that!"

This from me,— a word by the way,— very sure
that no matter what assertion I cover by that name,
it will be received by him for truth. There is something very beautiful to me in the pride and heart-
felt love which the men so often express for their
generals. It is this feeling of trust and confidence
in their leaders which is one of the most important
elements of success, and upon which victory itself
often depends.

Ah! here comes M. We have been wondering
where she could be, and why she did not appear.
Her hands full, as usual, and stopping for a Christmas Eve greeting with each man, as she comes
along. And see who she has brought in her train!
Men and boys laden with green wreaths; more
still? we shall have quite a bower; and look at
that great tree; where can that have come from,

and what can she mean it for? It has been given
to her, she says, and we may' use it exactly as we
like best; therefore —— suggests that it shall be
a Christmas tree for James, who has just announced
his intention to hang up his stocking, and she pro-
poses this in its place. We all take it up as an
excellent joke, and declare he shall have it. He
seems to enjoy it too, and smiles with that sweet
smile, which I am sure first won his young wife's
heart, though I should be sorry that she saw it now,
with that weak, languid eye and pallid brow; we
must put a little color into those cheeks, before we
send him home. Having nothing else to do, this
busiest day of the whole year, —— promises to
supply all the needful, for dressing the tree, when
she returns from dinner, says goodbye, and leaves
the men all in high spirits.

The work goes briskly on; some of the men
have got tired and left us, but most of them are
faithful still, especially my friend there,—that tall
Yankee, with his crutches laid at his side. He is
a New Hampshire man; and, with true Yankee
perseverance, has never moved since he concluded
to try his hand at "greening letters," as he calls
it. He "calculated he could do that as well as
anything else, though he had never tried before,"
and wonderfully has he succeeded. Many a merry
laugh rings out, as the different ones hold up the
results of their work to know if we have an idea

"what that letter is intended for?" and truly we often find some difficulty in recognizing them, but trust their position in the sentence may be more suggestive than when they stand alone. It is tough work, and I am almost inclined to agree with one of the men, who, as he puts the last stitch to his work, starts up, exclaiming:

"Well, any man that can do that work, is fit to go back to his regiment; I've done nothing like it since I left the Peninsula."

As we are hurrying on, to meet the constant demands from the dining-room, "Can't you give us an E?" "Isn't that A done?"—a quiet little man at my side turns to me, and says, in an under tone:

"No one thinks of the poor fellow who died here this morning," pointing to the bed directly back of the spot where our merry group is gathered.

"Died here! To-day? Who? When?"

"Just about a couple of hours ago. A man you never saw; only brought in a few days since."

Could it be possible that here, where we had all been so full of mirth and gayety, but a few hours since, on this very spot, on this Christmas Eve, too, a soul had passed from earth—from its vigil here—to keep the Festival—where? None knew, and none can ever know, till the Awful Day, when "the secrets of all hearts shall be revealed."

There was a special sadness about this death. I

found, upon inquiry, that the case had not been considered a serious one; that the man had even spoken of being at home on New Year's Day; that the ladies had brought him a drink that morning, which they had prepared for him; and scarcely half an hour later, the wardmaster, in passing, had been struck by his appearance, went up to him, and found him quite dead. Apparently he had died calmly and without struggle; this seemed more probable from the fact that those in the nearest beds, even, had no idea of it; but there was a loneliness about that passing which I could not forget.

Had he felt the dark cloud coming ere he entered into its shadow? Had he longed to speak—to call —and had no power? Had he yearned to send one last message—one parting word of love—to those far-away dear ones? We may not know; and if a tear moistened those bright greens, as they lay almost upon the spot where he so late had been, was it not a type of earth, and of the constant mingling of earthly joy and sorrow, from which we may never escape long as we linger here?

> "Sorrow and gladness together go wending;
> Evil and good come in quick interchange;
> Fair and foul fortune forever are blending;
> Sunshine and cloud have the skies for their range."

I have dropped my work, and am dwelling sadly on these thoughts, when I see one or two start up, and rush over to James. What is it? They are lifting him from his chair, and placing him upon his bed. Ah! it is one of those terrible fits; and see, four men are holding him down. Here comes the doctor; let us move away all this work, and keep him quiet. Is it our fault? Have we tired him by our noise, and thus brought it on? Oh no! the doctor is consoling; he does not at all attribute it to us; he has them often, only he must be kept quite still; and goodbye to all hopes of his Christmas dinner in the dining-room to-morrow. The usual remedies are applied, but it is a severe attack, and leaves him utterly prostrated.

We all repair to the dining-room, and here is, indeed, a scene of bustle and confusion. Ladders against the wall, men putting up the half-finished sentences, festooning the green wreaths, hanging the flag in graceful folds, so as to dispose its bright colors to the best advantage amidst the greens, hurrying in and out on various errands, and busying themselves about one scarcely can tell what, only all adding to the general confusion and excitement. Can any one wonder that no sad impression can continue where there is so much to turn the attention and divert the mind? We are conscious ourselves of its influence; and, of course, men, in whom the feeling is not a deep one, must be much more open to it.

But here is ——, with all her promised parcels

11

for the Christmas tree; how sorry she is to hear of poor James' fit; but we decide that it will be best to make the tree for him, and have it placed at the foot of his bed to-morrow, to atone for the loss of the dinner; not to-night, the doctor forbids all excitement at present.

And now, here is the tree, but how shall we plant it? Some suggest one mode, some another; but none take it in hand, till our ever-obliging Corning, wardmaster of our first ward. appears; prompt to do, and ready to act, he wastes no time in words, but bears off the tree, and soon returns with it firmly planted and ready for service. Thank you, Corning; what a satisfaction there is in being so promptly and pleasantly served. And now we have hands enough. —— unfolds her treasures, and wondering eyes and busy hands are soon occupied with them; and ere long the tree stretches out its green arms, laden with golden glories of gilt balls, soldiers in every conceivable costume, pocket mirrors, which may yet look upon more warlike scenes than those they now reflect,—in fact, decorations of all sorts, suspended by red, white, and blue cords, and glittering gaily in the gas light. Ah! here is an addition; thank you, Lawrence; those bright red apples, which he has just washed and polished, will have quite a fine effect, as he is hanging them among the other miscellaneous specimens which this wonderful tree produces.

We are all satisfied and delighted with it, but the great drawback is that poor James cannot see it, now that it is done; but Price, his wardmaster and faithful nurse, has promised to lift it in, and place it at the foot of his bed, in the morning, and we know that he never neglects a promise.

The Chaplain is to hold a Christmas Eve Service here, this evening at seven o'clock; so we are anxious to have everything in order; and really, it all looks very nicely, and we regard it quite complacently, as we take a final survey of our day's work. That star, which —— brought with her, covered by kind hands at home, shines out beautifully, surmounted by the green cross; and our Lectern holds up its head, quite proud of itself in its Christmas vestments.

But now, we really must wind up, for the night has come; and with mutual good wishes for to-morrow's enjoyment, we say goodnight.

As for the day itself, I can give you little account of that, as, of course, I could not be present; but the dinner was described to me, in glowing terms, by those who were.

The turkeys, the pies, the plum-puddings; the toasts that were given and drunk with " three times three" in beer, generously given for the purpose,—in fact, everything seemed to have passed off "a merveille;" but the best part of the whole, was the orderly manner in which it was conducted —not a single case reported for the guard-house. This pleased us especially, as it seemed to prove that our efforts for the men's enjoyment had been attended with no bad results, and to make the remembrance of our Christmas of 1862 one of the bright memories of our hospital experience.

May God grant that ere we hail its dawn again, those now in rebellion may have returned to their allegiance, and thus enable us to proclaim a blessed peace throughout the land. But there is something first. Before Peace must come Prayer. We need Prayer; the nation needs Prayer.

Do not point me to the little band of people or parishes, where the Daily Offering is made,—where throbbing hearts, and souls yearning for the safety of their loved ones, daily kneel before God's altar, and in lowliness and penitence send up that pleading wail, which seems as though it must pierce the very Heavens, and cleave a pathway to the mercy-seat:

"O, most Powerful and Glorious Lord God, the Lord of hosts. that rulest and commandest all things; Thou sittest in the throne. judging right, and therefore we make our address to Thy Divine Majesty, in this our necessity, that Thou wouldest take the cause into Thine own hand, and judge between us and our enemies."

And again:

"Hear us, Thy poor servants, begging mercy, and imploring Thy help; and that Thou wouldest be a defence unto us against the face of the enemy."

Most thankful am I for this, and for all that we have, little as it is; but I am now looking at our country as a whole.

We know the South to be wrong; we know ourselves, or rather, our cause, to be right. If, then, we have right, truth, and justice on our side, why do we not succeed — why have we not succeeded?

Is it not that we have been — we are — a sinful people, pluming ourselves upon our powers, priding ourselves upon our prosperity, till we have come to look upon the fair beauty of this land, lavish in its loveliness, as a possession which is our right, and not as a loan, for the use and enjoyment of which we are bound to return the offering of grateful hearts?

Is it not that we have gone on in a suicidal career of extravagance, luxury, and dissipation, which has finally brought its own punishment upon us? Sorely did we need humbling, and sorely have we been humbled. Bitter has been our lesson, but bitterly was it needed. The thought will sometimes arise, would that the trial had come from foreign foe; would that friend had never lifted hand against friend, nor brother against brother!

11 *

Had that grand rising, at the sound of Sumter's wrong, which swelled throughout the North—had it, I say, but thrilled through our whole land with a mighty throb, till, with one heart and hand united, we had joined to defend that Flag, so treacherously assailed, where is the foe we should have feared to face — where the enemy, which, humanly speaking, we might not have conquered?

But so, the lesson had been lost. We had but gained further food for pride, further motives for self-glorification. The medicine would but have increased the disorder, the remedy added to the disease. We must acknowledge — we must recognize the Chastening Hand which is dealing with us. Where is the victory which has ever yet, as a people, sent us to our knees? Where the defeat which has ever yet been attributed to any but secondary causes? Want of reinforcements, want of supplies, want of suitable weather, want of skill in the commanding officers,—any and every want but the true one.

We send our men forth wanting the one weapon, which, springing from its scabbard, and flashing in the bright sunlight of Faith and Trust, must insure success. It is the Sword of Prayer.

> " 'Tis Prayer that moves the silver bowers afar;
>   Gains wings, and through the ever-opened door,
>   Swift as the image of the twinkling star,
>   Shows its reflection in the Ocean's floor;
>   It moves the inmates of that Heavenly Shore,

As, gently rippling o'er the leafy shade,
Comes the soft, sighing gale, and passes o'er;
E'en so in Heaven, each Prayer, in secret made,
Ruffles a thousand Wings prepar'd for instant aid."

I humbly beg pardon, dear C. You asked for some account of our Christmas festivities at the hospital, and I have been betrayed into what, I fear you will find, a tedious expression of my feelings upon the questions which have such an absorbing interest at the present time. Forgive me this once, and I will promise to spare you in future.

POOR JOSÉ!

"But these men have no feeling."

THE stormiest day of this stormy winter. Hail,
rain, and snow seem to have formed a precious
triumvirate to take possession of the day, "vi et
armis," and claim it for their own. I know not
whether it is a certain perverseness of nature, or
a desire to overcome difficulties, which leads me to
prefer such blustering, battling days, to more serene
ones; whatever may be the cause, the fact will
account for my finding myself, on this particular
morning, seated on the kitchen table, before the
hospital fire, carrying on a *warm* discussion with
one of the men, on the merits of Ruskin, as I dried
my dripping garments. A chance word led to a
quotation by him from one of Ruskin's works, and
we immediately "opened fire" in more senses than
one.

I found him a man of keen intelligence, self-
made, of course, but a great reader, and quite
familiar with a higher style of literature than we
usually look for here. Doubtless, in his far-away
home, grander halls have echoed to the praises of
the great Art-teacher of the nineteenth century,

made by more appreciative critics; but I very much question whether he has ever had more earnest, zealous, enthusiastic admirers than the two that day met, before that kitchen fire, on the shores of another continent.

As I walked through one of the wards, a little later, I said, in passing, "You are better to-day," to a man who had been suffering from such a severe attack of erysipelas in his head, that his eyes had been closed for many days. The enormous swelling of his head, added to his long, matted beard and thick, tangled black hair, had given him a fierce, brigand sort of air, which was far from being dissipated by the appearance of a pair of large black eyes, opened to-day for the first time since I had seen him in the hospital.

"Better," said he; "but oh, lady!—"

He turned his head away, shaking it sadly.

"What is your grief?" said I, sitting down beside him.

"My little ones, my little ones! Where are they? Five weeks, dear lady, have I lain here, and no word have I had from them."

A long, and most sorrowful story followed, of which the main points are these: a Spaniard by birth, he had come to this country in search of employment, settled in Philadelphia, married, and for several years was prosperous and happy, till his wife fell into bad habits, wasted his earnings,

and brought them to utter poverty and wretchedness. On one occasion he had gone to a neighboring town on business, and on his return found their
comfortable home broken up, the house and furni-
ture sold, and his wife and their three little ones in
a poor hovel, in one of the worst parts of the city.

No one who did not hear him, can imagine the
pathos with which he described his little girl's
illness, with all the fervor of his warm Spanish
nature; his care of her; his walking the floor with
her night after night, her little arm around his
neck and her head upon his breast; "for you see,
lady, it was worse than if she had had no mother."
His love for her seemed to amount to a passion;
his boys, he said, were "nice little fellows," Juan
and Henriquez; but evidently his feeling for them
was nothing in comparison with the idolatry
lavished upon his little Rosita, as he called her,
a child of four years old.

"I lie here at night," said he, the large tears
rolling down his cheeks, "and think if I could just
once have that little hand in mine, that little head
upon my breast, it would cure me faster than all
this doctor's stuff, far away faster."

From what he told me, I gathered that he had
enlisted in the war in despair; and during his
absence his wife, for her outrageous conduct, had
been considered insane, and taken to the insane
department of the almshouse, where she then was,

the children having been taken to board by a woman in the neighborhood of their house. He had been unable, as he had said, to hear anything about them, and feared they were ill, especially his darling Rosita.

"Lady, dear lady, could you, would you see about them for me?"

"Certainly," said I; "if it is possible, I will go at once; but I must first know where they are."

"You will?" he said, "You really will?" with an expression of wondering delight; and then, as though the very thought brought peace, remained perfectly still, apparently musing upon the idea.

"But," said I, "you do not tell me where to find them."

"No —, —— Street."

I started, and shook my head. "That is impossible; I could not go there."

"Impossible!" he said, his voice amounting almost to a shriek. "Don't say it! Go, dearest lady, go! Nothing could hurt you; God will protect you; oh! go. I would kneel to you if I could rise."

"I do not want you to kneel to me; I would go at once, but it would not be right."

"Not right! not right!" he said, with utter despair in his tone. "Oh! then what on earth can be right?" and covering his head in the bedclothes, he groaned as though from the depths of his soul.

As this is no autobiography, it matters little by what train, either of reasoning or of cars, I reached the spot where I stood, an hour later; nor, for the same reason, shall I be more particular in my description of what followed, than is necessary for my narrative. Suffice it to say, a certain account of "St. Margaret's court," in the matchless poem of Aurora Leigh, was before me, stereoscoped into life, never again to be mere word-painting.

A little, low, blue frame building; the outer room, into which you step from the street, is apparently a small green grocer's shop. Strings of suggestive-looking sausages hang in ropes from the top of the door and window; pieces of black-looking material, yclept bacon, by courtesy, are piled up among barrels of gnarly green apples, evidently not gathered from the gardens of the Hesperides; baskets of eggs — which I am very sure no tidy hen would ever confess to having laid — crowd the little, low, dirty counter, behind which stands the live stock of this interesting apartment. And certainly the object upon which my eyes first rested did not belie her "entourage." It has been well said, that the soul makes a harmony for itself in its surroundings, and thus character is developed and declared. If so, how beautifully the unities were here preserved; for why should we not have the unities of dirt, as well as those of elegance? Doubtless that Celtic soul found as much enjoyment in seeing all around her in such perfect keeping with her own appearance, as Beau Brummel ever did in the appointments of his famed boudoir. I should almost have hesitated to ask a question of this curious production of nature,— something between a crone and a hag, with coarse Irish features, loose dress, hair hanging down, and apparently guiltless of any tending of either comb or brush since she had attained maturity, which was certainly not yesterday,—had she not herself opened the way.

"Get out of this, will you, *Jewann*, don't you see the lady?" addressed to a dirty, commonplace-looking little urchin, of about nine years old, who sat tilting himself forward and back upon the edge of one of the aforesaid barrels, with infinite peril to life and limb. This rather remarkable name, with her felicitous rendering of it, seemed to me circumstantial evidence, and I gathered courage to ask, "Are you the person who takes care of José's children? I have come to see them for him."

"Yes, miss, walk in; we've but a poor place, as you see. Rosy, come speak to the lady."

But it needed not the name; as soon as my eyes rested on the child in the corner, I was satisfied that this was her father's darling; and who could wonder at his love! Rarely have I seen a more

12

perfect specimen of "beauty unadorned"—the rarity of the jewel enhanced and thrown out by the coarseness of its setting. She lifted her eyes from the floor, on which she was playing, to stare at the unwonted visitor—large, liquid, Spanish eyes—with that expression of love and confidence in them which seldom outlives childhood. Those tangled black curls, her father's pride, were almost hidden beneath a common, coarse, little worsted hood, in which she had stuck four or five chicken feathers, which gave her a sort of picturesque air; a large stain of the dirt in which she was living, rested on one cheek; but it seemed merely a shadow bringing out the bright tints beneath.

"Come here, Rosy, I say, and speak to the lady; she's just seen your pappy."

At that word she sprang up, and came wonderingly to my side, never taking those eyes from my face.

"Yes," said I; "I have just come from him, and he wants so badly to see his little Rosita; what will she send him?"

In a moment her little arms were tightly clasped round my neck, as I bent down to speak to her, and those rosy lips were pressed to mine, in a warm, loving kiss.

Quite aware that this mute message, eloquent as it was, could scarcely be delivered with satisfaction to any of the parties concerned, I drew one of the feathers from her cap, and said, "Shall I tell him his little girl sent him this?"

A bright, beaming smile, was the only answer I could extract. The woman now began a piteous story of having to provide for them — no money, etc., etc.,— backed by her husband, who appeared, pipe in his mouth, from some back den, evidently hoping to extort funds; but when they discovered that I was in possession of all the facts, with regard to the support of the children, they seemed to find it useless to proceed; and finally agreeing to my request that one of them would take the children to see their father, I left the direction, visiting days, etc., with them.

Once more I stood by that bedside, which I had so lately left, with that deep groan ringing in my ears.

"Do you know what that is?" said I, holding up the feather.

No answer from the lips, but the eyes said, plainly, "I don't know, and I don't care."

I varied the question. "Do you know where that came from?"

He started, pierced me through with those keen black eyes, then said, seizing the hand in which I held it with a grasp which secured my remembering him for many days, "You didn't?—you couldn't? —it isn't?"

"Yes," said I; "I drew it from your little girl's cap; she sent it to you with her love."

His grasp relaxed; and, burying his face in the pillow, he sobbed aloud. I waited, thinking he would recover himself, but no word came; hard, heavy sobs, only increasing in violence, shook the bed, and I was frightened at the terrible emotion I had called forth. Deeming it best not to notice it, I began quietly to give him an account of my trip, dwelling on the least exciting parts of it, but all of no avail; apparently he did not even hear me, and I saw that he was getting entirely beyond his own control.

What was to be done? Here was indeed a dilemma. He was exciting the attention of the whole ward; it was within half an hour of inspection when the surgeon in charge goes his rounds through the wards,—what would he say? Was this the way that the ladies excited their patients? But beyond and above all, he was injuring himself; and with the tendency to inflammation in his head, I dreaded the effect of such strong excitement, and yet all I said seemed but to increase it. Suddenly it occurred to me that (something on the principle of "similia similibus curantur," little as I usually admire the practice) perhaps by evoking another feeling equally powerful, I might calm him; and knowing that no one, be it man or woman, will ever submit quietly to blame without an attempt at self-justification, I changed my tactics at once, and said:

"How it is possible, that a father, who has one grain of love for his children, can permit them to remain one day, or hour, in such a den as that, is to me a marvel that I cannot comprehend."

The rûse was a perfect success. Starting up in his bed, with flashing eyes, he said, with a vehemence which at another time would have frightened me:

"How cruel! I couldn't help it, and you know I couldn't; haven't I told you how it breaks my heart, night and day, to think of them there, and I tied here and can't get them away?"

This was all I wanted; he poured forth a volley of eager self-defence, and ere it was half over, my mind was quite relieved about him, and I had the satisfaction of seeing him in a short time quite composed, and anxiously seeking to know every particular of my visit. He would not be content without hearing over and over the most minute details, all the time stroking and patting the feather, as though it were indeed the little one it symbolized.

The following Sunday, as I passed through the ward to attend service, I saw the three children on the bed; the two boys seated at the foot, and the little Rosita lying on his breast, with that dimpled arm round his neck, as he had wished.

12 *

He smiled as he saw me, and held up the feather.
I never saw him again. I heard, the next time
that I came to the hospital, that news had been
brought him of his wife's death at the almshouse;
he had been allowed to go out on a pass, but had
failed to return, and nothing further had been heard
from him.

Poor José! We shall, in all probability, never
meet again on earth; but I can never think of him
without finding, in his history, the most powerful
proof that " these men *have* feeling."

ROBINSON.

"WAR is an unmixed evil; look at it as you will, it is, it must be, an unmixed evil!"

This, in an indignant tone, from one, standing at my side, gazing at one of its saddest results.

"An evil, I grant," said I; "unmixed I deny. War and its attendants have a grand side. Do not start, and look so reproachfully at me; were we standing on another spot, and were the circumstances different, I would tell you all I mean; but let it pass."

We were in no mood for argument then, and the subject dropped; but it recurred frequently to my mind, and the more I have dwelt upon it, the more I am convinced (your pardon, dear speaker!) that such a statement is not, cannot be true. War has its compensations, its beautiful compensations; and I very much question, whether, if the statistics of the good deeds, the kind, warm, large-hearted actions, could be registered, as are those of crime, we should not find that those performed in times of war, greatly overbalance those in times of peace. Great crises call forth and compel great deeds.

Where is the battle-field since Sumter's sad surprise, which cannot boast, not one, but many Sir Philip Sydney's, with the earnest "Take it; thy need is greater than mine?" Magnanimity need no longer be confined to the field of Zütphen, and each child be taught the story as though it stood alone. Where the hospital where we may not see something of sublimity in the beautiful forgetfulness of self, the untiring devotion with which plain, poor men watch, night after night, by a dying comrade,— a stranger till those walls had made them brothers? Where the home, high or humble, which fails to show the brave-hearted wife, mother, daughter, or sister, giving for her country a life far dearer than her own, to danger and to death? Is there no moral grandeur, no moral heroism here? A sad soul, so struggling with, yet surmounting sorrow; so sending forth her sure support and stay, then turning calmly and quietly to take up her lonely cross and bear the burden of daily life, by virtue of such act reaches a spiritual elevation which times of peace could rarely, if ever, witness.

I see the laugh — I hear the cutting remark, "Such a *woman's* view!" but I know these things are true, for I have witnessed them; and, be it remembered, that ridicule is not reasoning, nor satire always sound sense. Never can I listen to this statement, that "War is an unmixed evil," without longing to combat it; and added to that, but this very morning, the same belligerent desire was excited in my mind by reading an opinion, somewhat dogmatically asserted, that, "In these days, Apollo must give place to Mars."

"Not so," I answered then; "not so," I answer now. Apollo never gathers in a heavier harvest— never stores stouter sheaves, than those mowed down by the chariot wheels of the God of War, as he dashes onward in his headlong career. Ask the world, since creation's dawn, and she will tell you that Apollo clings to Mars; and if he ever "gives place," it is only that he may follow on the fiery track of his great leader, sure of grander opportunities in the waxing and waning of one moon, than a life-time of peace could give.

And even granting (which I never will) that Apollo pauses in his course—that his lyre "lingers o'er its lays"—are not the daily deeds of our loved land, at this moment, prouder poems than this continent has ever yet produced? Where can we find such stirring strains, such ringing rhythm, such burning ballads, such lyric lays, such sublime sonnets, such ever-during epics, as these times of ours call forth? Is not each soldier a poet in his way? And shall his verse have the less power, for that it is set to martial music? Shall it touch our hearts the less? Rather, shall not every chord vibrate ten thousand times the more, for that the pages on which it is written are the fair fields of our own dear country; its pen, the sword; its ink, the heart's blood of our brothers?

But I have wandered wide of my mark. I seated myself to note a simple story, of one of that ever-growing army who have nobly given their young lives to their country.

I have made allusion before to my whistling friend, Robinson, who was brought to the hospital at the same time with our poor Darlington, from the same regiment, and wounded in the same battle, —that of "Fair Oaks." His left arm was terribly shattered, just below the shoulder, and injuring the shoulder-blade; and for a long time his case was a very critical one, requiring the most close and constant watching. He was entirely confined to his bed for many tedious weeks, and yet I know not why I should apply that term to the time so passed; for they were certainly never "tedious" to us, although we felt great anxiety for him, and we never had any proof that they were so to him. Patient and uncomplaining, the only sign he gave of suffering, save the contraction of his brow, was the constant effort to whistle away the pain, and his moans in his sleep. There was always something inexpressibly sad to me in these moans; it seemed as though the body were compensating itself, during sleep, for the powerful restraint imposed upon it during waking hours.

I have rarely seen greater unselfishness in any

one. During his illness, it was all-important to keep up his strength, for as the wound began to heal, one abscess followed another, and kept him much prostrated; we therefore tried to tempt his appetite in every way; and often, when I have brought him some delicacy, he has pointed me to some one near him, with the words, "Please give it to him; he cares for such things more than I do."

His love for his mother, and anxiety to spare her all unnecessary suffering on his account, was very beautiful, and attracted me to him from the first. His weakness was so great that he was utterly unable, for a long time, even to feed himself, and of course, could not write. When I offered to do so for him, he declined, saying, that she knew, through a friend, that he was here; and that the sight of a strange hand, with the conviction that it would bring that he was too ill to write for himself, would be worse for her than to wait for a little while.

One day, some time afterwards, I came to his bedside and found a paper lying there with a few unmeaning scratches, as I thought, upon it; he held them up to me.

"The best I could do."

"What were you trying to do?" said I; "did you mean that for drawing?"

A look of intense disappointment passed over his face.

"I was afraid so," said he; "then it would frighten her, as I thought. I meant it for my signature, and I've looked at it, and looked at it, and hoped it didn't look as bad as I thought, at first; but if you ask what I'm trying to do, when you see it, the game's up, and it's no use."

I assured him that such a signature would be far stronger proof of the real state of the case, than any letter I could send telling the facts, and giving the reasonable ground for hope which we now felt. But he still preferred to wait; and ere very long we found, by pinning the paper to the table, to keep it firm, he could execute a tolerably legible epistle. The weeks rolled on, and, by slow degrees, he regained his strength; his bright, hopeful disposition, even temper, and uniform cheerfulness, were great aids to his recovery; and we watched his improvement with great satisfaction, and at last had the pleasure of seeing him able to be up, and even out, for a short time.

He came to me, one morning, in our ladies' room, saying, "Miss ——, would it be troubling you too much, to ask you to write to mother?"

"Brought to it, at last!" said I. "Why do you ask me now, Robinson, when you have refused so often before, and can write for yourself?"

"That's just it; she won't believe what I say;

thinks I'm fooling her, and pretending to be better than I really am; and has an idea they're going to take my arm off, and I'm keeping it from her; and I thought if you'd just write, and tell her it wasn't coming off, she'd be sure to believe you."

"Sure to believe a stranger in preference to her own son, Robinson? Does that tell well for the son?"

"Yes, ma'am, I think so; she knows you could have no object in deceiving her; while the thing I care most for in the world, is to keep her from fretting, and she knows it."

There was no combating this reasoning, and in a short time I received a beautiful answer to my letter, well written and well expressed, confirming all that Robinson had told us:—That he was the youngest son, and had always been carefully and tenderly brought up; that he had two brothers, the only other children—one had gone to Texas, before the breaking out of the rebellion, and never having heard from him since, they feared he had been pressed into the rebel service; fortunately she had never heard, and I trust, now, never may hear what Robinson had told us,—that, while pressing on, at the battle of Fair Oaks, over heaps of the enemy's dead, he saw an up-turned face on the field, wounded or dead, he knew not which,—that face, he said, he never could mistake—it was that of his brother!

We tried to convince him that this was most

13

improbable — that his imagination was excited at
the time, and that the dread that such a thing
might happen had been "father to the thought;"
but in vain; we never could persuade him to the
contrary; and yet, whether from a doubt in his
mind, or the dread of the pain it must cause, he
never, as we afterwards found, had made any
allusion to the subject in his letters home.

One morning, after he had been able to be about,
and even out for some weeks, I was surprised, on
going into his ward, to find him in bed again.

"Why, Robinson, I am sorry to see you there!
What have you been doing?"

He hesitated, twisted the end of his coverlet, but
made no answer.

"Nothing wrong, I'm very sure of that.   It
wasn't your own fault, was it?" said I, fearing
he thought I doubted him, as so many of the
relapses here are caused by excess, the moment
the men are able to be out, and I well knew there
was no such danger here.

He looked up at me, at once, with his clear,
honest eyes, and said, "Yes, Miss ——, all my
own fault; but I thought *she* worried so——"

"Your mother?" I questioned.

"Yes, ma'am; and if I could just slip my arm
into my coat-sleeve long enough to have my picture taken, she'd see it was better, and it would set

her mind at rest more than all the letters I could write."

So to satisfy this mother's heart, the poor wounded shoulder had been forced into its sleeve, giving him, as it did, several weeks of added suffering and confinement to his bed. Can any one wonder that such a man should have won his way to our hearts;—or at our regret, when we found he was to be transferred to another hospital, at some distance from the city? We thus lost sight of him for many months. Several times when I asked after him, at our own hospital, I was told that he had been there but a short time since; sometimes the week before; sometimes only the day before; but it so happened that we never met. His wound, they told me, was far from well, varying very much; some days giving hope that it would heal, and then bursting out again. I had received many and urgent letters from his mother, before he left us, begging me to use all the influence I could bring to bear, to have him transferred to a hospital near his home; (this was, of course, before the present order on that subject had been given) but on applying to the surgeon, I found that he considered his wound far too serious to attempt the journey, and that Robinson so fully agreed with him, that I wrote the poor disappointed mother to that effect, trying to console her with the hope of restoring him to her, ere very long, perfectly

cured. The winter slipped away; the pressure
of present hospital duties and interests had almost
crowded out all thoughts of Robinson, when I am
surprised, one sunny April afternoon, to receive a
note from one of our lady visitors, telling me of
Robinson's extreme illness, and that it is scarcely
supposed he can recover.

An hour later finds M. and myself driving rapidly
out to the hospital where he now is; and here we
are at the gates; how shall we enter! Ah! we do
not now fear a guard with a bayonet, as we should
have done some time since; and fifteen minutes
more suffices for all the necessary "red tape" connected with admittance, and we are at the door
of Robinson's ward, listening to the wardmaster's
answer to our question :

"Yes, ladies, walk in; but he won't know you;
he's too low, and he's flighty all the time."

"Wont know us!" Robinson not know us! We
cannot believe that; but see! he is leading the
way; and we follow to a bed where lies a man
tossing restlessly, and talking, or rather muttering
to himself in an indistinct tone; his bandaged
shoulder and arm resting on a pillow, for an operation has been performed — a large piece of bone
extracted—and the result still doubtful. Doubtful?
No; too certain; that face is enough. Poor mother
in your western home, you can never look upon
your boy, till you meet at the final Bar, in the

presence of your Judge! God in his mercy grant
that it may be to spend a happy eternity together!

And yet, as we stand, we find ourselves almost
doubting whether this can really be our merry,
laughing, whistling Robinson. Little hope, indeed,
that he will recognize us, but let us try.

"Robinson, do you know me?" He starts, and
in a moment the vacant gaze changes into one of
his old bright smiles of recognition.

"Know you! Why shouldn't I know you? How
long it is, Miss ——, since I have seen you,—and
you too," added he, stretching out his hand to M.;
but even as he spoke, his expression changed, and
his mind wandered again.

And this was the end of all our care — this the
result of so many weary months of suffering. He
seemed pleased at our coming, and would answer
any direct question, but could not sustain a conversation of even a few moments. We found our
old friend, "handsome Harry," of concert memory,
who had been transferred at the same time, established here as Robinson's devoted nurse, although
entirely unable to move without crutches. He told
us that the surgeon had told him that morning,
that if his family wished to see him, he had better
telegraph for them at once. Robinson heard us,
and catching the word "telegraph," said quickly,
"Don't telegraph; father's poor, and he might

13 *

come on; I'll be better soon, and get a furlough, and go out to them."

"But, Robinson," said I, "you are very ill; perhaps you may not be better, and you would like to see your father."

"I don't think I'm very ill—they said so to-day; but I think I'll come round soon."

The next moment he was on the field, and evidently going over the fatal "Fair Oaks" fight.

His friend Harry told us that it had been his most earnest desire and longing to see his father; and that he had urged him, some days ago, if he should be worse, to let them know at home. I therefore wrote the telegram on his table, and we drove to the office on our return to the city, that no time might be lost.

I was detained at home for the two succeeding days; but some of our ladies went out to see him each day, as he was a general favorite; one lady going in a pouring rain, although she knew that she would have nearly a mile to walk after leaving the cars; their report of the case was most unfavorable. On the third day, the Rev. Mr. ——, who had been a most constant and faithful friend to Robinson, in our hospital, went out with me. When we arrived, we found him in a terrible state of excitement; he had been talking, and was now almost shrieking, and dashing himself from side to side.

"It's no use speaking to him, to-day," said the wardmaster; "he don't know anybody."

But once again I tried it, and once again he extended his hand, and repeated my name, and then said, "And Mr. ——, how very kind in him to come!"

I sat down by him, and tried to soothe and calm that dreadful restlessness; his mind was too much gone for words, I only gently stroked his brow and fanned him. "I am out on the water; out on the water!" was his one cry, from a low tone, ascending till it amounted almost to a scream. Truly he was "out on the water," and where was compass or chart for the final voyage? Those words, with the constant repetition of his brother's name, were the last I ever heard him utter. The only moment of calmness I noticed, was when Mr. —— knelt at his bedside and repeated those soul-soothing Prayers, from the "Visitation of the Sick." He attempted no conversation, for we well knew Robinson was in no state to bear it. We had felt from the first, that Prayer *for* him, was all that we could offer; not *with* him, as his intervals of consciousness were merely momentary. His father had not yet arrived, and there appeared little hope that he could now do so, in time, as he was very much lower than on my last visit, and evidently sinking. As our presence could give him no comfort, we left him with heavy hearts.

When I reached there the next day, I found that an order had been given prohibiting all admittance for visitors to his ward, as the surgeon thought that Robinson had been excited by those he had seen the day before, but that his father had come, and that we could see him; he had arrived that morning.

There are few things connected with this hospital work which I recall with more pleasure than the simple, earnest gratitude of this bronzed and weather-beaten old man, for the trifling kindnesses which we had been able to offer to his boy. There was something about him altogether so real, so honest, genuine, and sincere, that one could not help feeling drawn to him at once. He was a rough, plain, Western man, primitive in the extreme; but no one could listen to him without the consciousness that a warm, true, noble heart, beat beneath that uncouth exterior.

Had the telegram been a day later, he could not have reached here for nearly a week longer. The train, which only runs on certain days, left the morning after he received the news; he had travelled night and day, making every connection, and performing the journey as rapidly as it could be done.

His boy, he said, had recognized him, and he was pleased to find him better than he had hoped for. He thought with care he would get well now, and

he was going at once to telegraph the good news to
his wife.

We were thunderstruck; how could he be so
deceived? For although we had not seen Robinson that day, we well knew he was in a condition
from which he could not rally. It seemed therefore
no kindness to allow his mother to be tortured with
false hope, and we earnestly represented (hard as
it seemed to do so) that the surgeons did not look
for any improvement; but all in vain,—he had seen
sickness—he had seen doctors mistaken before now
—his boy was going to get well; so he accompanied
us to the telegraph station, and sent his message.
That evening I was told some one wanted to see
me, from the —— hospital, and on going out, was
met by the words, "Miss ——, my boy's gone, my
boy's gone!" and a burst of sobs, which seemed
as though it must shake that poor old frame to
pieces.

He had scarcely left, in the morning, to send his
hopeful telegram, when the change took place, and
Robinson breathed his last just as his father reached
his bedside. The blow fell heavier, as we had feared,
from the strong hope he had persisted in entertain-
ing, and even then it seemed as though he were too
much bewildered and stunned to realize fully what
had occurred. There was something inexpressibly
touching in the grief of that poor, bowed-down old
man, shattered as he was, too, by hard travel and

loss of rest; and yet I hardly knew how to comfort
him, or to answer that sad appeal, "How can I go
back to his mother without him?" Deep grief
must ever bear with it a reverence of its own, and
this seemed something one scarcely dared meddle
with.

He said the funeral was to take place the next
afternoon, and begged that the ladies who had been
so kind to him would be present for his mother's
sake; he thought it would comfort her to know it.
I readily consented, and promised to inform the
others.

He rose to go, and drawing a little paper from
his pocket, said, "I thought maybe you might care
for this; it is a lock of my boy's hair, which I cut
off for you, and I thought his mother would be
glad to know you had it."

I expressed my feelings in a few words, which
seemed to soothe and gratify him.

That poor mother seemed never out of his
thoughts; and again and again would he repeat
that piteous question, "How can I go back to her
without him?"

But he need not have feared; that mother's heart
was anchored on the Rock which alone can with-
stand the storms of earth. Listen to but one
sentence from her first letter (to one of the ladies,
who had been a kind and constant correspondent,)
after that sad return.

"At first it seemed I could not bear it. My bright-faced, joyous boy—my sunbeam! But soon came the thought, how short the journey would be for me to go to him, and that my sunbeam would now shed its ray upon me from the sky, to light my path onward and upward."

It would be of little avail, to go into the dreary details of that dreariest afternoon. Touching in the extreme did it seem to see the little band (for the ladies willingly agreed to the request to be present) take their places as mourners, with the father; mourners in reality, though so lately strangers; mourners, for we claimed a right to grieve; for was it not, as I have said, a young life, given for our country as well as his?—for the one common cause, which forms so strong a bond between all loyal hearts?

A heavy, pouring rain added to the general gloom; the only comfort came from the words of our Burial Service, which must always fall with blessed balm upon the sorrowful soul. It was performed at his father's request, and with the permission of the surgeon in charge, by Robinson's kind and true friend, the Rev. Mr. ——, to whom I have alluded before.

It was a long, long time ere I could forget the face of that broken-hearted old father, as—every-thing over—he stood at the door, as we drove off, leaving him lonely and desolate among strangers.

He was to start that night alone, in the rain, on his sad, homeward journey, and seemed to long to keep us with him to the last; and how we longed to stay to comfort him! But we must say goodbye, and with a long, warm grasp of that rough hand, we parted, and one more hospital sorrow was over.

Brave, gentle, heroic heart! The aching limb, the suffering frame, the strained, excited nerves are stilled forever. Robinson sleeps in a land of strangers; but the turf that covers that "soldier's grave" will be moistened and kept green by the tears of those who can never forget that bright example of noble unselfishness, and beautiful patience under severest suffering and trial.

"I AM OUT ON THE WATER!"

U. S. A. Hospital, April, 1863.

Out on the water! No compass, no chart!
The sails all in ribbons; the timbers apart!
The vessel is tossing, the storm driving fast,
Out on the water; nor rudder, nor mast!

Out on the water! The dark night hath come;
The ocean is boiling and seething in foam;
We see the waves break o'er the poor battered boat,—
Out on the water; a soul is afloat!

Out on the water! Quick! reach him a spar!
It is not too late, drift he never so far;
Hold to it! Cling to it while the waves toss,
Out on the water,—the Spar of The Cross!

Out on the water! Is't harbor at last;
Are "the waves of this troublesome world" safely passed?
We pray, through That Spar, that the soul hath made Port—
That, out on the water, The Cross was Support.

THE RETURN TO THE REGIMENT.

A BRIGHT, sunshiny week. Moral sunshine, I mean; for like St. Peter's, at Rome, our hospital may be said to have "an atmosphere of its own"— our brightness or dulness being in a great measure dependent upon the state of our patients. Deaths, or very severe cases of illness, naturally have their effect in casting a shadow on everything around; but at present, most fortunately, we have nothing of the kind; and our principal grief (though in a very mild form) has been from the daily partings caused by the return of our men to their regiments; which, from some unknown cause, seems to have been the sole business of the last few days. The "Hegira" has been going on steadily through the whole week, and we have been busily occupied in helping to stow treasures into impossible spaces in knapsacks, slipping in some little contribution of our own, to call up, perhaps, a smile of surprise when opened far from here; in putting up lunches for the travellers — for it has happened that some of our brave boys have fainted on the way from exhaustion produced by delay in getting their meals; therefore, by the surgeon's orders, they

14

are always provided when they start—and finally, in bidding them "Goodbye, and God speed!"

This returning to regiments has amounted to an epidemic this week; the contagion is spreading rapidly, and it is very plain that Dame Example has, in this case, been exerting herself for good. She has taken some of our chronic cases by the hand, lifted them out of bed, and made them feel that effort and firm resolve will do more for them than yielding to the languor of a slow convalescence. One may ask, "Is it, then, at the option of the men, when they shall return to their regiments?"

"Most certainly not."

"Does not the surgeon decide that point?"

"Most certainly he does."

The surgeon of each ward makes out his list of men fit for service, and hands it to the surgeon in charge, who in his turn examines the men so reported and returns them to their different posts; but, as we all know how much the mind has to do with the body, men who have seemed quite unfit for duty, often, under the stimulus of one of these departures, rouse themselves, make an effort, and find that a little exertion was the only thing needed to fit them for their work. But, on the other hand, this strong desire sometimes carries them too far; a case in point occurred this morning.

"Why, Shaw, my man! out of bed to-day? I'm

glad to see you up; you'll soon be off, with the other boys."

This, from the cheerful voice of one of our surgeons, to a man who, from a long fever, had been too feeble, for many months, to do more than sit up in bed for a short time.

"That's just it, doctor; Pat's going to-day, and I can't let him go without me. I think I could bear it, maybe. Won't you let me try?"

I noticed a slight look of surprise on the doctor's face; he pressed his finger on the man's pulse, was silent for a few moments, and then said, kindly:

"Perhaps you can go with the next lot; stay out of bed, to-day; try to walk a little about the ward; eat more, and I've no doubt you can go back soon; but we should have you back on our hands, were we to send you to-day."

"But Pat, doctor? You see we're from the same town; he's young,— only a slip of a boy — and I promised his mother I'd see to him. I did let him get hit, to be sure, but it wasn't much to signify; my fever was a good bit worse; we were brought here together, and I'm bound to leave when he leaves, whether I can shoulder a musket or not."

How glad I was that it happened to be just that particular surgeon to whom he made his appeal; for it must be admitted, even in this pattern hospital, that skill and sympathy, power and patience,

knowledge and kindliness, are not always combined;
but in this instance I was very sure the decision
would be given (whatever it might be) in a manner
which could not offend; nor was I disappointed.

" Well, my friend, if you had told me that you
had kept Pat from getting hit, I might have taken
it into consideration, whether, for the sake of Pat's
mother, it might not be my duty to return a man
to his regiment who can't walk across this hospital;
but as, by your own account, you let him get hit,
I think you'll have to trust him without you, and
wait here till you're a little stronger;" and kindly
patting him on the shoulder, he laughingly turned
off.

Poor Shaw! It was a sense of duty — certainly
not any feeling of ability to go—which led to the
proposition; for as the hope departed, his strength
went with it. He attempted to rise from his chair
at the side of the bed, tottered, and would have
fallen; but I saw it, sprang forward, caught him,
and threw him backward on the bed, knowing I
had not strength to support him.

" I didn't mean to knock you down, Shaw, though
it looks a good deal like it," said I, as there was a
general laugh, amongst those nearest to him, who
witnessed the proceeding.

No answer. The effort had been too much for
him—he had fainted. I called an orderly to bring
me water quickly, and bathed his temples from

the cologne bottle in my pocket, but he did not revive.

"What's the fuss?" said one, coming up behind me.

"Miss —— has knocked the breath out of Shaw, that's all."

"And he's knocked the color out of her; she's whiter than he is."

"Don't talk; get me some water," said I, hastily.

"La! miss, you're not really minding, are you? He always has them turns when he tries to sit up; and he's gone a good bit, and we don't mind, he'll come round; he's been fretting at little Pat, there, going without him, and wanted to go back to his regiment with him. Fine hand at a march, wouldn't you be, eh, Shaw?" said he, as the latter opened his eyes.

With rough kindness, he put his hand under Shaw's head, raised it, and held the water to his lips. Shaw roused himself, looked round, and seemed gradually recalling what had occurred.

"Drink, old fellow! and you'll soon come round. It's my advice to you, to stay in your bed till you're fit to get out of it; you ought to be ashamed to make a lady look like that."

"Be quiet, Gilman," said I; "I'm not frightened at all; I've seen worse sights here than a fainting man; it was only the effort of suddenly throwing him backward, which I felt for the moment."

14*

But I have no doubt Gilman's rebuke was of far more service to Shaw than my ready sympathy would have been; for it roused him, and diverted his mind from his own sorrows. He did not at all know what he had done; but was profuse in bewildered apologies for some unknown wrong to me, which he seemed to feel convinced that he had committed; although the " how, why, or what" was wrapped in mystery. I soon satisfied his mind on that point, and then, more guardedly, touched upon " Pat;" promised to see to his comfort as far as possible; give him good advice as well as good food,— little doubting which would be the more welcome,— and finally, promising Shaw to return as soon as they were off, I hurried away, fearing I was already too late to say goodbye.

These partings are brighter things for those who go, than for those who remain; it is as true here, as in other cases, that " Les peines du départ sont pour celui qui reste." The bustle, the excitement of getting off, the hope of service, the prospect of change of scene, make the going something pleasant, even to those whose patriotism is not at fever heat; while, for those who remain, the sight of others going, the consciousness of their own inability thus more painfully forced upon their minds, the sense of confinement, make the hours after one of these departures a somewhat sad affair, and we have to exert all our powers to restore cheerfulness.

A bustling scene meets me at the door of our room. A busy group is crowded there; some kneeling on the floor, strapping knapsacks and blankets; some jumping into the well known blue overcoats, which have enjoyed a profounder rest than their owners have done since their entrance into the hospital; some settling their caps well down over their eyes, as though cap and "caput" were never again to part company; while some (yes! they really have,) have begun to say goodbye. M. calls me, and I hurriedly enter.

"They're going; you'll be too late to see them off."

"Hurrah, boys! Come on. We're off. Goodbye, ladies! We won't forget you. If ever the rebs come here, send for us; we'll stand by you, and fight for you, too."

"Goodbye, ma'am, if I get hit I hope they'll send me here."

"We've had a bully time here, and we're proper sorry to go back. 'Salt horse' and 'hard tack' will come pretty hard, after all your nice little messes. Goodbye, ladies, and thank you kindly for all you've done for us."

Such are the parting words, rough it may be, but coming from the heart, and therefore far more valuable than the elegant insincerity of more polished partings. But as character is shown in every action of life, we may easily detect the

difference of nature even in their mode of saying
goodbye. One comes forward with frank smile,
and hand extended, his whole soul beaming from
his honest eyes; he is glad to have known you,
somewhat sorry to leave you, but so very happy
to be off, that there is little room for any other
feeling; and you take leave of him with satisfaction, sure that his contented nature will adapt
itself to whatever circumstances may surround
him. Another comes up really sorry to go, but
thinking it beneath a soldier's dignity to show
feeling; he therefore tries to assume a perfectly
indifferent air, but like everything assumed, it sits
ill upon him, and we all know that in his heart
"sober Sam," as the boys nickname him, is more
sorry to leave us than he cares to acknowledge.
A third shocks our patriotism by openly declaring
he don't want to go; he don't care to fight, and
he's sure he's not fit for it either. Ah! Bob, isn't
it that you love your own ease a little too well?
The field may not be quite so comfortable as it is
here, but it is unworthy of a soldier to mind such
trifles as want of bed, and occasional want of food.
But Bob doesn't think so, and whatever his other
faults may be, he is honest in declaring his opinions.
But here come the others, and we have but a few
minutes more.

"Goodbye, Brown; take care of yourself; we
shall miss you when we want our errands done."

" Goodbye, Williams ; don't forget your promise."

" Goodbye, Simpson ; what shall we do without you for a wardmaster?"

" Goodbye, John ; come back with shoulder-straps, and God bless you!"

That bright young face looks still brighter, as he says, " Why, Miss ——, that's what they all say to me; I've been through the wards bidding the boys goodbye, and they all say 'God bless you, John!' Why do they say that to me?"

I could have told him without much difficulty why that genial, sunny nature, so full of bravery and beauty, of life and love, had won its way to the hearts of " the boys," and called forth that warm " God bless you." The Prayer from so many hearts seems to have won its answer; God has blessed him and guarded him from harm. Nobly has he fought, and the shoulder-straps are won. Promotion on the field " for distinguished services," has been gained; and we now have the pleasure of directing our quondam " Private " John's letters, to " Captain " John, of the Army of the Potomac. But as he is pressed on in the crowd, before I can answer his question, I notice a pale, quiet youth, always retiring and gentle, standing at my side with a hesitating air.

" Well, George, you're off too; I won't forget you, and you mustn't forget me."

He still stands, and still hesitates, saying nothing.

"Can I do anything for you, before you go, or perhaps after? Can I help you? tell me."

"Yes, ma'am, you can help me. If you would just let me shake hands with you, I think it would help me on the battle-field, to remember it. I saw the others come up, but somehow I didn't dare to, and I was so afraid I would have to go without."

Poor George! Not many of the men are so troubled with modesty. Such a little boon to be asked for so earnestly! one, too, which half the men claim as a right in parting.

"You didn't think, George, after all our talks, I could have let you go without shaking hands with you, did you? No, my boy," said I, holding out my hand; "but I will do what will be more likely to help you on the battle-field, pray for you; and now, goodbye."

He grasped my hand, and as he held it, a hot tear fell on it; he seemed shocked, dropped it, and rushed from the room into the crowd waiting at the door to start. The signal sounded, and they were gone.

"God go with them!" said an earnest voice at my side.

God will go with them! Doubt it not,
    Ye, whose fond, aching hearts
Fear that your treasures are less safe,
    Because from you apart!
Love, human love, is powerless,
    From Death or harm to shield;
Our very lives, for theirs laid down,
    Could no protection yield.

God will go with them !   Rest on that,
    When partings make Life dark ;
He guideth every bullet's course,
    To hit or miss its mark.
Then trust them amid shot and shell,
    To His unfailing care;
And bow, submissive hearts, howe'er
    The answer comes to Prayer.

A VISIT TO THE WARDS.

U. S. A. HOSPITAL.

AND so you really wish, dear C., to take that long-promised trip through the wards of our hospital? Most happy shall I be to escort you; and I promise, ere we start, to use every endeavor to prevent you from going any deeper than you wish into the "horrors of hospital life." You shall not see an open wound if I can help it;—do not imagine that I have forgotten the effect upon you of the sight of that man's arm the last time that you were here; and yet it was your own fault, for it was your expression of interest in him and his wound which led to the display; and we, hardened creatures that we have become, were not aware of your feelings till the harm was done. But put yourself under my guidance to-day, and I will pick out only the choice specimens. Yet no! I cannot do that exactly, for, in answer to a charge brought against me here a few days since, I have promised to select the worst cases — the *morally* worst cases, I mean,— in the hospital, to show my friends. What was the charge? you ask. Nothing very heinous, to be sure. A friend, to whom I have very often talked of the hospital and its inmates, said to one of our medical cadets, as we walked through the wards:

" Tell me, doctor, is a hospital really the paradise Miss —— represents it? Her soldiers are all perfectionists; they never quarrel, they never swear, they never drink, they never gamble; and more than this, they never get well; they are sure to die in some romantic way, with an interesting wife, mother, or sister, in the distance."

My answer, of course, was a laugh, trusting to my friend, the cadet, to justify me; but here I was mistaken. His answer was a mere empty word of compliment, as to what the ladies made the hospital, etc., leaving the main question untouched. I therefore was compelled to take up my own defence, and assure her that the fact of my having preferred to dwell upon the interesting cases, was no proof that the hospital contained no others; that we all knew that either in or out of a hospital, our strongest feelings were called forth by extreme illness and danger.

> " Like a bruised leaf, at touch of Fear,
> Its hidden fragrance Love gives out."

More than this, that here, as elsewhere, people ceased to be interesting when they recovered; therefore, most naturally, I had not dwelt much upon such cases as had returned, cured, to their regiments. I further assured her that I had heard

15

men both quarrel and swear; had seen them both
drink and gamble within these walls; and that, at
the very moment we were speaking, a special friend
of mine—acknowledged to be the worst man in the
hospital—was in the guard-house; a man who probably interested me more deeply and painfully than
any one here; and whose story, could I tell it, might
thrill her to her soul's depths; but in this case also,
there was an "interesting mother in the distance,"
whose pale, patient, long-suffering face, mutely
appealing to me from her sweet photograph, must
seal my lips forever upon that sad subject. Because
I had told her that oaths were checked in our
presence, did it follow, I asked her, that they were
never uttered in our absence? Because I had said,
and most truly, that in my whole term of service
I had never heard a rude word, or seen an act of
discourtesy, either to myself or any of the lady
visitors, did it follow that such words or acts never
passed between themselves? Because I had shrunk
from the painful theme of the guard-house and its
inmates, did it follow that it was untenanted? And
finally, triumphantly made her confess that, like too
many amongst us, she had formed her conclusions
on insufficient data, promising, as a reward for her
generosity in owning herself routed, that henceforth I would reserve the pleasant cases for myself,
and pick out the worst ones for my friends, as they
seemed to prefer them. I tell you this, that

you may understand why I take you, first of all,
to the crossest man here, in preference to the most
attractive and gentle. You do not care to see him,
you say. Oh! yes. For the sake of my promise
I must show him to you, and after that we can
look at pleasanter specimens. He will not hurt
you; it is only that nothing that can be done for
him ever suits him, unless done by the ladies; for
he is no exception to my rule, and is always polite
to the ladies. Amongst ourselves we call him "The
Grumbler," so entirely that we sometimes forget
his real name. I was amused, the other day, to
hear M. say, as she designated the different saucers
of corn-starch which she was giving to one of the
orderlies, "You'll remember, now, that this is for
Davis, that for Strickland, that for Jones, and this
for 'the Grumbler.'"

"For who, ma'am, this last one, did you say?"

"The Grumbler," repeated M. with perfect un-
consciousness, as she continued to hunt spoons
for the different saucers.

I quietly enjoyed the bewilderment of the
orderly, but said nothing to enlighten him.

"That's what a good many of them are, ma'am,
when I goes back without enough for all, but I
don't know which one you mean now."

M., thus recalled to herself, laughingly explained;
and the idea that such was the ladies' name for him,
seemed to afford special delight to the poor orderly,

who has doubtless been frequently the victim of
his wrath.

"You've hit it this time, ladies; he does nothing
but grumble from morning till night; nothing that
I can do will suit, though I've tried till I am tired,
to please him."

Whether he has confided to him our flattering
name for him or not, I have not yet been able to
discover, but think it not at all unlikely. As we
pass along to his bed, just notice the tables of the
men, and see how carefully they have the "Lares
and Penates" treasured up on them.   Pictures
of wife, mother, and sister, little remembrances
carefully preserved; the Bible,—often the parting
gift — and once or twice a little toy, which seemed
to keep home fresh in the father's heart; but one
thing has often struck me with surprise; these all,
as you may see, lie open on the table, but you will
never see the bride elect — the promised one — so
exposed; her memory and her face are as carefully
guarded as though she were in danger of being
captured and carried off by storm.   I have seen
quite as much reserve and delicacy of feeling upon
this point, as I have ever met with in higher circles.
The story comes at last; but it is often after months
of watching and nursing, when you fancy every
detail of home has been given over and over again,
— it comes in bashful words and with heightened
color, " I thought I'd like you to know;" or, " You

won't mention, will you?   But "—and then comes
confession.   Or again, a sudden burst of gratitude
seems to find vent in showing you that precious
one, so carefully hidden all this long time; and a
photograph is mutely placed in your hands, and
of course no *woman* ever yet said to any picture
so given, "Who is this?"   Ah! well.   I fear you
are tired, long ere this, of my earnest desire to
prove that the human heart is the same all the
world over, prince or peasant, baron or beggar,
senator or serf; so let us walk on, and speak to
our cross friend.

There he sits, on that bed opposite to us, in the
red shirt, with his arm in the sling; that's a bad
wound, and I often excuse his irritability, because
he is suffering so much with it, and I know that
the doctor thinks amputation may be necessary.
He is a good-looking man, if he would only smile
and look good-natured, instead of frowning and
scolding all the time.   There comes his dinner;
now listen, but don't go up to him, just yet; if
he sees the ladies, he won't express his views so
plainly.

Grumbler, loquitur.   "Call that my dinner?
Pitch it out, I say, pitch it out, or I'll pitch you
out!   Didn't I tell you the next time you brought
me that greasy stuff you call soup, I'd report you?
say, didn't I?"

Down-trodden orderly, rising at last.   "Pitch it
15 *

out yourself! The other boys can eat it; I don't see why you're so mighty nice."

"Mighty nice, indeed! I tell you it's grub not fit for an almshouse, that's what it is."

Let us go up and speak to him; perhaps the sight of the ladies may allay his wrath.

"What's the matter, George? what are you speaking so violently about?"

"I beg your pardon, ma'am; I didn't know you were there."

"But the whole hospital might have heard you; and I just want to know, for curiosity, whether you really referred to that chicken soup, when you said it was "grub fit for an almhouse?" because, if you did, I want to tell you that I have just finished feeding a very sick man with it, and that, as I tasted it before giving it to him, I thought how nicely it was made; and that, tired as I was, I should not object to have a little ordered for me."

"It's that coat of grease on the top, ma'am, that I can't stand; it makes me sick, and I've told him over and over not to come near me with it, big fool that he is."

"But, George, it's very easy to remove that; it's been standing, that's all; look here, just take your spoon, and skim it off; there, see how nicely it looks below. Do you know I think you're something like that soup yourself, crusty and disagreeable on the surface, but skim that off, go deeper, and I don't believe you're such a bad fellow, at heart, cross as you seem!"

"Why, do I seem cross, Miss ——? I don't mean to be so, only they never bring me what I want; and this plaguey arm keeps aching so all the time."

"That's just what I thought; and I am sure that if we could only get that arm better, you would be a different man. I am sure you suffer with it a great deal. Try and take this nice corn-starch, maybe you'll like it better than the soup."

"That! Old scorched stuff! You won't catch me taking that in a hurry, I guess."

"Scorched? Why, George, it isn't scorched."

"Not scorched, ma'am? No milk, pretended to be boiled, ever came out of that kitchen yet, that wasn't scorched."

"That, I happen to know, is not so; but just tell me one thing,—have you tasted it?"

"Not I, and I don't mean to; I know it's bad, without tasting it."

"Thank you, George, for your gratitude. We made that this morning, with our own hands, with particular care, and put the flavoring in it you said you liked the other day; it has never been near the kitchen, and I can answer for it's not being scorched."

"You made it, ma'am? The ladies? Then it's

the kind I like. I beg your pardon. Billy brought
it in with the dinner, and I thought he got it out
of the kitchen."

"We sent it to you by Billy; but, if it had come
from the kitchen, wouldn't it have been as well to
try it, before condemning it so strongly? I feel
much mortified that this lady, who has come to
see the hospital, where we try so hard to have the
food nicely prepared, and delicacies provided for
the men, can go home and tell that she herself
heard one of them say, when his dinner was
brought to him, 'Pitch it out,' for it was 'grub
not fit for an almshouse.' You ought to be careful
what you say, George, for perhaps you do not
know what is the fact, that the testimony of the
men, with regard to these things, outweighs tenfold all that the surgeons or the ladies can say. I
constantly hear the remark, 'Oh! yes. Of course
it is to the interest of the surgeons to represent
that everything is as it should be; the ladies are
proud of their hospital, and of course praise it;
but ask the men,— they are the ones to tell the
truth about it—ask them if they are comfortable,
and get what they want; if they are satisfied, be
sure it is all right, and vice versa.' Now, this lady
has come in, and you know what she has heard, as
the testimony of the only man she has yet listened
to. Is this quite fair, George?"

"Oh! Miss ——, I'm very sorry, indeed I am.

I didn't mean it, you know I didn't; only this plaguey arm, as I tell you, keeps me snappish-like."

"Well, never mind, I don't think you've done much harm this time; this lady shall taste both soup and corn-starch, if she will, and then she can bear her own testimony that the one is not greasy, nor the other scorched. Only grumble a little less next time, and we will forgive you now. But come, dear C., we are wasting too much time on one case, and there are so many here that I want you to see."

Ah! here comes one of our finest specimens, a whole-souled, true-hearted man; one whom you may safely trust, and never fear that you will find your confidence misplaced, which, I am sorry to say, is not always the case. You shake your head, and mean by that, I suppose, that a man looking as well as he does, certainly might go back to his regiment. I grant you that he looks per-fectly well, but let me beg you not always to be guided by appearances here, any more than else-where. Some of those we have supposed best fitted for service, were really the least able to bear exertion. I remember a case last winter, which taught me a lesson on that point. Corning, one of our men, who was afterwards made ward-master, and whom I have often mentioned to you as one of my favorites, is the one I have in my mind. When he first came to us, he was suffering from a severe kick from a horse, which had broken several ribs; but after a few months he appeared so perfectly well, that we used very frequently to take the liberty of judging, and wonder why he was not returned to his regiment.

One afternoon, during a violent snow-storm, he undertook to join one or two of the men in a game of snow-balls; that evening, when we were preparing the suppers for the sick men, Corning failed to appear as usual for his ward, and we found that the exertion of the afternoon had been quite too much for him; he was in bed, and for weeks was not himself again. This showed me how thoroughly unfit for any but the lightest duty a man might be, and yet appear—as our friend here does—in good health. "Our Charlie," as the men call him, is a general favorite; he was one of our orderlies, and has just been made wardmaster, and has proved very popular in that capacity. He has one of those sunny, genial natures which create an atmosphere of their own, and brighten every one who may chance to come within the sphere of their influence. Poor fellow! he was giving me an account, yesterday, of rather an unfortunate picnic which he was at the day before. A party of the men had obtained passes to go upon one of those excursions which are so popular here in summer; he had foolishly taken with him his pocket - book, containing thirty dollars ("John Greenback," as they irreverently term the pay-master, having paid the hospital a visit the day before), which in a very short time he found he had lost. He had been sitting on the grass, with a set of men all of whom were known to him except one, whose appearance he had not liked when he joined the party; this man, who had just left them hurriedly, he felt convinced had taken it. On giving notice to the police, he was advised to say nothing, but keep a close watch, and he would probably be able to detect him.

"It wasn't the money I cared for, a bit, Miss ——," said poor Charlie, in telling me of it, "but the pocket-book had *that paper* in it, and you know that was more to me than all in Uncle Sam's treasury."

I well knew what "that paper" meant, for it was through it that we first found out what a true, loving heart beat in the breast of our bright, frank, off-hand Charlie. His brother, also in the army, had been wounded, brought here to another hos-pital, and died there while Charlie was here, without his knowing it. With that thoughtful kindness which has brought comfort to many an aching heart during this sad war, one of the ladies pre-served a lock of his hair for his family; and hearing, after all was over, that Charlie was here, brought it to him, and gave him all the particulars of his brother's death. No one, who had once heard Charlie give that account, could ever forget it; the deep, bitter sorrow, which refused to be comforted; the unavailing regret — almost self-reproach—with which he wound up, "And to think I was so near, and never went to him!"—this seemed to be more than he could bear.

We always found ourselves more ready to sympathize with him in his grief, because he entered into every one else's interests so warmly, whether of joy or sorrow. "That paper," therefore, I knew contained this precious lock of hair; which, he told me only a few days ago, he wanted to send to his mother,—"all she can ever have of her boy"—and had delayed doing so, only because he wished to give it to the chaplain to send for him. It needed no words of his, to tell me what a loss this was to him. Later in the day, however, as he was walking through the grounds, he saw the man whom he had suspected, seated under a tree with a woman,—who afterwards proved to be his sister, and to whom, they found, he had given one-half of the money. Notice was given at once to the police, who immediately arrested both of them. On being detected, the man instantly put a roll of notes into his mouth, and tried to chew them up; this was speedily prevented by the policeman, who throttled him and compelled him to disgorge them. "But," said Charlie, "I begged

him not to choke him, as I wanted to hear where
the pocket-book was, much more than to get the
money." This, however, the man obstinately refused to return, nor could it be found upon him
after the strictest search. "After telling him what
was in it, too," continued Charlie, " after begging
and beseeching him by the love of his own mother,
just to give me the pocket-book, and keep the
money (evidently, from what he told me, to the
infinite disgust of the policeman), could you believe me, that he wouldn't listen to me, but walked
on, just as if he didn't hear me? As we went
along, I saw him suddenly pitch something over
a fence at his side; a thought darted into my mind;
over that fence I dashed, and sure enough, down
there in the grass, was my little white paper; and
now they may keep my money, and welcome." It
seemed to perplex him terribly, where the paper
could have been concealed during the search, or
how the man happened to have it out of the pocket-
book; but such was the fact, just as he related it.
He told me that the police had been at the hospital,
that day, bringing him fifteen dollars,—half of his
money — which the sister had confessed that her
brother had given to her at the time, and requiring
him to go and give evidence against the man, which
he was most unwilling to do, having, as he said,
" secured all that he cared for."

But while I am making a long story of Charlie's
16

loss, you are looking eagerly at that bed in the corner; that poor fellow, who is so pale and languid, is from Wisconsin; he has injured his spine, and cannot sit up for more than a few moments at a time. He is one of the mournful ones, and our most earnest attempts to cheer him seldom produce more than a feeble smile. Nothing could convince you more of the blessing of buoyancy of disposition and a sanguine temperament, than a short time passed in one of these hospitals; you see at once that it carries a man more than half the way towards cure. But nothing we can do will brighten poor Granger; he seems gentle and grateful, but persistently depressed, and that makes us feel much discouraged about him. You are looking at the gentleman sitting at his side; yes, it is, as you think, Mr. ——, one of our most valuable aids here; he has, for many months, been assisting the chaplain in visiting, reading, writing for, and talk ing to the men, and most grateful do we all feel to him for his services here. No sun too hot, no air too heavy, through this whole summer, to find him at his post; and the men repay his kindness with the warmest attachment.

Look at this man just coming in at the door; it is poor Cuthbert; he does not belong in this ward, but he wanders where he likes. His is a sad case. A bullet struck him on the head, injuring his brain; at times he is perfectly himself, but usually his

mind seems quite gone; it is truly pitiable to see
him. His wife and little children are here in the
city; she tells us that he was a most industrious,
faithful workman, before he enlisted; honest and
sober, and the kindest husband. We are very sure
of his unselfishness, for no matter what we brought
him to take, whilst he was confined to bed, his
answer was always the same, " Give it to Bob;"
or " Bob's wounded, give it to him." He rejected
everything for himself with these words, fancying
himself still on the field with his friend. We found,
to our surprise, that " Bob " was none other than
young Lieutenant ——, well known here, whom he
had been nursing and watching most tenderly till
he had received his own wound. The news of
" Bob's " death, which reached us soon after we
arrived, would doubtless have been a great sorrow
to him, but the poor fellow never could understand
it; and we begged the men to say nothing about
it, during his sane days, as we all wished him spared
this additional suffering. He will get his discharge
soon, but his poor wife will now have to support
him, as well as her children. Surely a Soldier's
Home, for those disabled by this war, is one of the
charities most imperatively demanded at present.
I know that efforts are even now on foot to obtain
it, but it is a thing which should, which must, be
pressed. Why pause till we see it accomplished,
and those suffering and thrown out of employment

for life, provided with a home? Why rest till we have actually placed within its walls the army who have returned—many of them in the prime of life —maimed and mutilated, to our midst—cut off from all possibility of advancement for the rest of life—helpless, and too often hopeless? Shall we not show them that we can at least appreciate all that they have done for us?—that we can, and will gladly deny self, to give to them the home which their sufferings and self-sacrifice have so deservedly won? We need but the earnest purpose to secure its fulfilment, and I cannot feel that Philadelphia will ever rest till she has added to her generous labors in sending men forth, a liberal provision for the comfort and maintenance of the disabled, on their return.*

Let us pass down on this side, as we go out of the ward. I want you to look at that man's eye, it is so full of bright, keen intelligence and quick wit. I wish that we had time to talk with him; but it is such a difficult matter to break off, that, without an abundance of time, I always hesitate to begin. The other morning I happened to enter the ward just as inspection was over; (which, you know, means the time at which the surgeon in charge makes his rounds attended by the surgeons of each ward;) this man beckoned me to his bedside.

* This was, of course, written before the establishment of the "Soldiers' Home," at the corner of Crown and Race streets.

" He's a bully man, that head one, ain't he?"

Criticism from the men upon any of the officers of the hospital, be it favorable or unfavorable, is a thing which we strictly discountenance at all times; and I therefore said,—assuming, or, as —— says, I should always say, *trying* to assume, an air of dignity—

" You should not speak so of the surgeon in charge, it is disrespectful; you must remember that he is as much your superior officer, for the time, as the colonel of your regiment."

" Faith! then there's an act of disrespect I'll never pay my colonel. He's gone to his account, so we'll say no more; but not a boy of that regiment will ever——"

This I could not permit; so I turned at once to leave him, finding my moral lessons turned against myself, and that " hæc fabula" didn't " docet" the respect I intended.

" Oh! please, miss! don't go—don't be offended! I didn't mean it, indeed; I may be rough, but I mean no offence; I want to tell you why I called him ' bully;' just let me, even if you don't like him."

" It isn't that I don't like him," I endeavored to explain, "but that I think you have no right to criticise those above you. Were I to allow that, I might, on the same principle, allow you to find fault with one of the other officers; I never meant that you should not be grateful for being so well cared for."

16 *

"That's just where it is, miss; it don't matter the being cared for; they cared for me in Washington; but it's the way the caring's done. I'll just tell you how it is, in this war. We're all a set of ten-pins, stood up to have balls sent at us; along they come, and down we go. No matter, get another set; but still, it may save Uncle Sam to mend the broken ones, and use them again; so the menders come along, pick you up, feel you all over, and see if you're worth mending; if so, you're patched up, and stood in your place again. I've seen enough of it; but here comes this fellow — I beg your pardon, miss, it's surgeon in charge I'm thinking you like him called — and he don't say much different from other menders; but it's all in his eye — it says a lot more nor his tongue — it says, 'You're flesh and blood, you are, poor fellow! and I'm sorry to see you twisting about with pain like that, and it's all a bad business, this same, so it is.' Do you think I care what a man's tongue says, when his eye says that? I tell you, I feel better the whole day for one look like that. It's my belief that all the talk that's right from the heart comes out of the eye, and when men want to make you believe things not just so, it's their tongue they use."

I did not suggest that it had been remarked, on the one hand, that "Language was given to conceal a man's thoughts;" or, on the other, that

" Countenance and gesture are vehicles of thought, but their capacity and scope are limited," as I was quite sure that he was entirely innocent of any plagiarism, either of ideas or their expression. But what a lesson in his words for us all! Here is a man confined to his bed, suffering acutely, who tells me that he feels better for a whole day — for what? For some kind act to relieve that suffering? —some pleasant look, or sprightly game to beguile his tedious hours?—or for

> " Kind words, so easy to speak,
> But whose echo is endless?"

For none of these; but merely for a look—a glance of sympathy! Could we realize the priceless value of such seeming trifles, surely in our intercourse with our fellow-men, we should be more on the watch to practice them — more prompt in their exercise. It is not that feeling is wanting, in many cases, but perception,—the perception of the mode in which we act upon others; but we must beware of forgetting our responsibility on this most important point, and remember that

> "Evils are wrought by want of thought,
> As well as want of heart."

Look at that man stooping down and playing with Dick, our hospital pet. A gentleman? you ask, and I cannot wonder that you do. Every one who sees him says, "But he isn't one of the privates?" He is; but I imagine there is no one

here more anxious to flourish in shoulder-straps.
He has interested me much since I first met him
here; he was very sick when he came in, but I did
not see him until he was better, and taking his
place as one of the orderlies—as our rule is in the
hospitals, that convalescents turn into wardmasters
and orderlies, before they are fit for active service
on the field. His deference to the ladies, and
certain little graces of manner, showed birth and
breeding; and I said to M. one day, "That man
was born a gentleman." I found that she quite
agreed with me, and had been struck by the same
thing. And yet there was an air of dissatisfaction
at times, and a bitterness of expression which I was
at a loss to account for. One morning I had brought
some books to the hospital, and on offering them to
him, amongst others, he told me that he had so
injured his eyes by over-study at college, that he
was unable to use them at all at present. A few
words more, and I discovered that he was a loyal
Virginian, who, on the breaking out of the rebellion,
had left family, friends, and a beautiful home, to
enlist in our army. All his relations were bitterly
opposed to the step; and he told me, with much
pain, that when our army was in the neighborhood
of his home, he had gone there to see his family,
but that they had positively refused to see him, or
even to allow him admittance. I could scarcely
wonder at his depression after this; but it seemed

to me that the consciousness of right, in the step
he had taken, should have brought him more content and peace than he seemed to possess. A few
afternoons since, he came in, as usual, with his
waiter, to carry the supper to the sick men (those
unable to leave their beds) in his ward. I noticed,
as I arranged the plates for him, that he looked
much disturbed, and that his hand trembled.

"King," said I, "you are hardly strong enough
yet to carry that waiter; you should ask one of the
other orderlies to do it for you."

I seemed to have fired a mine. Setting the waiter
down upon the table, he burst forth:

"It's no want of strength, Miss ——, but what
would you think if you saw Dr. —— and Dr.——
(naming two of our surgeons) playing wardmaster
and orderly in a hospital in the South? My position
was just what theirs is, and I chafe at this menial
work. My blood boils at playing waiter for the
men here; I can't stand it, and I won't."

I looked up in surprise. "What should I think,
King, should I see such a dreadful sight as you
suggest? I can tell you, very quickly, what I
should think. If those gentlemen had, for the
sake of their country, nobly given up every private
tie as you have done, and, by the fortune of war,
had been thrown into a hospital, I should honor
and respect them for fulfilling every duty there
imposed upon them; and I doubt not that they

would do it most cheerfully, as part of the service
their country asks at their hands. I should like
to know, also, whether it is less menial for the
ladies to turn cooks here, than for the men to
turn waiters? I cannot recall that I ever "chafed"
at the "menial work," or that my "blood boiled"
at cooking eggs, or boiling farina, unless on a hot
summer's day, when the fire seemed intolerable,
but never, I am very sure, from shame at the
occupation. We go even further, for we act both
cook and waiter. A day never passes that we do
not carry to the men what we have made for
them, to see if they like it — to know if it suits
them — or oftener still, to feed them, because they
are unable to feed themselves. Think what a state
of fever-heat our blood should be in at this time,
after two years of such services!"

"But the case," said he, "is not a parallel one.
Your service, grateful as we all feel for it, is volun-
tary, this is compulsory."

"I thought you were a volunteer, King? When
you enlisted, did you specify just the kind of work
you would do? When your country needed you,
did you limit the aid you offered? What matter is it
to you whether she asks you to fight for her, or to
serve her by ministering to her sick and wounded
members, suffering in a common cause from their
efforts on her behalf."

"I never thought of it in that light before."

"Think of it so now, my man; you will be far happier. That southern blood is a little too hot, and you have failed to perceive that all work is dignified and ennobled by the spirit which you bring to it. Because you are a classical student, and feel that you have talents and acquirements which fit you for something higher, you chafe at this service; but, believe me, the faithful performance of your duties here, will by no means unfit you for a command in the field so soon as your services there shall win for you the promotion you so much desire. So take up your waiter, and don't let your blood boil too much as you go up stairs, or you may upset my saucers."

He took my lecture in very good part, and since then we have been excellent friends. I think, since he realized that I preferred talking to him to lecturing him, and liked to enter upon higher themes with him, which he is so well fitted to discuss, that he has become more contented, and has resolved to accept his position. Let us speak to him; notice how his eye brightens and his expression changes, as he speaks.

"Well, King, how are your men to-day?"

"I've just been waiting for you, Miss ——; Joe sent me to ask you for two of those hand-splints you received yesterday—for the left hand, please—they are for Jarvis and Wright—those very bad arms, you know."

"Oh! yes. The splints that came with all those things, yesterday, from the Sanitary Commission. God bless that Sanitary Commission—what should we do without it? Our soldiers here have quite as much reason to be grateful as those in the field. Look at those shelves—all that wine, those jellies, preserves, syrups, and pickles, came from them, as well as these cushions, pads, and splints. They send us, constantly, fresh eggs, butter, lard, and such perishable articles as must be consumed at once. Here, King, take these splints, and then come back, will you, for some pickles I want to send to your men."

"Yes, ma'am, certainly, if I can get down again; but Joe is going away on a furlough, to-day, and I am to be wardmaster till his return."

"Shall your 'blood boil' more, or less, King, in your new position?"

Do you hear that merry laugh, as he goes up the stairs? No more fear for him; he is only making himself too useful, and we shall be sorry to see him returned to his regiment. Very tired, are you, of the study of character? I have about a dozen more men here that I should like to show you, but I will be merciful, and send you home, now, quite aware that you feel amply satisfied with your hospital diet to-day.

OUR GETTYSBURG MEN.

JULY, 1863.

IT is with peculiar feelings of gratitude, joy, relief, and safety, that we have entered upon our duties this week. The one absorbing idea of the last ten days—the impatience for the news of each hour as it passed—the eagerness to seek the opinions of friends, even though such opinions brought but further disturbance of mind — the difficulty of deciding upon the proper course of action.— the heavy, wearing anxiety — the slow realization that war, which we have, as yet, only looked upon at a distance, might, at a moment, be brought to our own doors,— our homes laid waste, and ourselves fugitives — all these things live too freshly in the minds of us all, to need word of mine to recall them. Who can ever forget the pressure which weighed down our spirits when we rose on that most memorable "Fourth" just passed?—the earnestness with which our cry to heaven went up for success to our arms — the pause of those long morning hours, when the whole city seemed holding its breath in terrible suspense — and then the grand, the glorious reaction, when the lightning

17

flashed peace and joy and safety to all hearts?
Did ever language bring more joy than those
two blessed words, " Meade victorious?" What
could we do but fall upon our knees, and offer
up our hearts in thankfulness for such an answer
to our prayers? God did that day "take the
cause into his own hands, and judge between us
and our enemies," and we were saved. Was it not
that, as a people, we had turned to him — as a
people we had acknowledged the weakness of a
human arm — as a people we had poured forth our
hearts in prayer, and he had heard us?

Those were indeed never-to-be-forgotten days.
Amid all other trials, came the sad thought of our
poor, wounded men at home. What would be their
fate? To leave them for the sake of personal
safety seemed so base; martyrdom for and with
them so attractive,—and yet it was not quite clear
to my mind—much as I longed to aid them—what
special benefit could accrue to them by self immo-
lation on the rebel altar. It was a difficult question;
and yet one always found payment for those anxious hours, in listening to the earnest promises of
protection and defence—so evidently sincere—from
those warm hearts; the wish and purpose so far
outstripping the ability.

" Don't you fear, ladies, we'll take care of you."

" We'll fight for you while there's a man of us
left."

"Yes, that we will! or a 'drop of blood left in our bodies."

"We'll make earthworks of our bodies before the rebs shall touch you, ladies, depend upon that."

"Only protect yourselves," said I, to a particularly valiant cripple, who had just expressed similar views for us, and slightly derogatory ones to the rebel general, then supposed to be approaching our city, "only protect yourselves, and I shall be quite satisfied."

"Protect ourselves!" said a poor fellow unable to move in his bed; "they'll make mince-meat of us, the first thing."

I found that this "mince-meat" idea took more firm possession of my mind than almost any other connected with the raid; and one of the greatest reliefs which I experienced on that joyful day, was the consciousness that it could not now be put into execution.

The afternoon of the "Fourth," as I entered the hospital, the beaming faces and glad congratulations of the poor fellows, proved how much they had dreaded the rebel invasion, in spite of the bold front which they had all presented, with the single exception of my "mince-meat" friend. I still recall, with pleasure, the intense delight of one man to whom I spoke of our victory. By some strange chance, which I never could explain, he had not heard it.

"Is that so? Is it really so? That's bully.
Let's do something!" and, nothing else being at
hand, he seized his pillow and sent it high into
the air.

But now come the sad results, which must follow
alike in the wake of victory or defeat. The wounded,
where are they? A battle on our own soil, and at
so short a distance from us, comparatively speaking,
must bring them to us more directly from the field
than any we have yet received; and we have been
hoping all this week, as they were pouring into the
city, that we should have our share.

"Hoping?" Yes, hoping; start not at the term,
I have used it deliberately. Once launched upon
the sea of hospital life, your views undergo a
change, and your one interest becomes to receive,
nurse, and watch the worst cases; it is the hospital
spirit, and you cannot breathe its air without im-
bibing the feeling. Monday, Tuesday, Wednesday,
Thursday, Friday have passed, with only the admittance of a few each day, none badly wounded,
and none requiring special care or tending; and to
those whose burning zeal makes them eager to pay
off some part of their debt of gratitude to men,
who, humanly speaking, have turned the enemy
from their doors, this is somewhat of a disappointment. We have had, to be sure, the pleasure of
several visits from old friends here, who had been

slightly wounded in the fight, and have been returned to other hospitals.

It is Saturday afternoon. I have just seated myself in our room for a moment's quiet, after a most busy, bustling day,—many sick, and much to do, although not exactly what we had wished for. M. rushes in, on her return from her dinner.

"Sitting quietly, I declare, as if nothing was going on! Do you know what's at the door?"

"Nothing different from usual, I presume; you needn't try to excite me; I've just taken a seat for a five minutes' rest."

"Go and look for yourself, then, if you are so incredulous. Ambulances and stretchers enough, I should think, to suit even your taste."

As I hurry, half doubting, to the door, I meet one of our surgeons, paper and pencil in hand, talking to one of the wardmasters.

"How many beds in your ward? All ready, did you say? That's right."

"Plenty of work for the ladies, Miss ——; I see some pretty bad cases coming in."

"Just what we wanted, doctor; we have been hoping they would come in our week, and it's almost over."

"Time enough, yet, to make them plenty of milk punch, and cold drinks. Some of them, I notice, are much exhausted, and will need stimulating."

17 *

Here was a practical suggestion—something to be acted upon at once, and far more useful than running to look at them, as they are carried in; so I return quickly, tell M. the doctor's wish, and all our pitchers are hastily filled with milk punch, iced lemonade, syrup and water, etc., etc. This, of course, occupies some little time; and as we reach the dining-room,—where all are placed who can walk, hobble, or crawl, till they are distributed into the different wards, while those on stretchers are being carried at once to their beds,— I almost start at the rough-looking set we suddenly find ourselves in the midst of. Are they miners or coal-heavers? Black enough and dirty enough for either; and I catch myself repeating over and over, "In poverty, hunger, and dirt," etc., till I am afraid I shall say it aloud. But what care we for dust and dirt? Set down your pitcher, shake hands, and thank them. Is it not Gettysburg dust and dirt? Is it not the dust and dirt of victory? Have not those torn and bullet-riddled clothes come straight from the field of their fame? And have they not saved us from distress, wretchedness, and ruin? I look at them with reverence; they seem to bring the battle so very near that the tears will rise, as those torn and dirty bandages show at what cost the victory was won. But do not imagine me standing all this time in a fine frenzy, meditating on the results of a battle. These thoughts slip in, between the filling and emptying of our pitchers, and the glad, grateful expressions for the "treat," as they call it. Poor fellows! they shall have our best, that is very certain.

As I am pouring out the last glass from my pitcher, my eye is caught by a face, on a stretcher, as it is borne past me. It is that of a boy, scarcely more than sixteen, I should think. His thick, black curls, eyes bright and sparkling, (with fever, it must be,) and brilliant color, contrast with his remarkably clean shirt and sheet. What can it mean, amidst this mass of dirt? As my work is done, I follow him into the ward.

"You can't have been in the Gettysburg fight, my boy, were you?"

"I don't know, ma'am, rightly, whether you'd call it in it or not; I was in an ambulance, in the rear. I've been in one, following the army, since the twenty-first of June; and it seems pretty good to be on a thing that don't move."

"But why weren't you left in a hospital?"

"'Cause I begged so to go on with the rest. The ambulance was going, and I begged them to let me go in it, and I promised to be well for the fight; so they took me; but I got so much worse, I didn't know when the fight was; it's the typhoid I've got, and my head's dreadful bad."

"Your hair is so heavy," said I; "we'll take

some of that off and bathe your head, and that will relieve it."

" Oh! no, ma'am; no, thank you; I don't want it off."

" Why not? It would be much cooler, and do you good."

" Why, I'll soon be well, and it looks so pretty when it's fixed!"

The time has come, since then, when I have quite agreed with David; those curls do look very "pretty, when they're fixed;" and I am glad he pleaded for them so innocently. Let no one ever say that vanity is confined to the breast of woman; the result of close observation has convinced me that it lives and thrives with tenfold greater power in man; and this little proof of it, just uttered with so much simplicity, only confirms a preconceived opinion. I do not, however, confide these views to my new friend, but advising him to keep perfectly still, I say goodbye, for the present, and pass on. As I hurry down the ward, I am struck by the expression of utter contentment and quiet, on a strange face—one of the new men, evidently; as I come up to the bed where he is lying, he seems to me to be actually *purring* with satisfaction.

" You look as if you were comfortable, my friend," said I, " even though you are not very clean."

" Oh! the blessing of this bed. If you could

know, ma'am, what it was to have been marching twenty miles, whether you could or not, again and again, you'd soon feel what it was to be put on a bed and let to stay there. Like the South, ma'am, I just want ' to be let alone;' I don't the least care whether I'm clean or dirty—I'm lying quiet, and I am happy."

"Well, after a bath and clean clothes, which they are giving the men as rapidly as possible, you shall lie as still as you please; but I am afraid that must come first."

"Don't think, ma'am," said he, laughing, "that I object to either of those things; they've not been too plenty where we were, but I just feel now as if I never wanted to move again."

"I can easily understand your feeling; enjoy your quiet as long as they will let you, and I will bring you some supper, later."

I left him and hurried over to our room, where I found M. busily employed, and hastened to take my share in the work. Just at this moment, as we were flying about in every direction, now here, now there, with a pad for one, a basin and sponge to wet wounds for another, cologne for a third, and milk punch for a fourth, I felt Dick (our hospital dog, my faithful friend and ally, a four-footed Vidocq, in his mode of scenting out grievances,) seize my dress in his teeth, pull it hard, and look eagerly up in my face. "What is it, Dick? I am

too busy to attend to you just now." Another
hard pull, and a beseeching look in his eyes.
"Presently, my fine fellow! presently. Gettysburg men must come first."

He wags his tail furiously, and still pulls my
dress. Does he mean that he wants me for one
of them? Perhaps so. "Come, Dick, I'll go with
you." He starts off delighted, leads me to the
ward where those worst wounded have been placed,
travels the whole length of it to the upper corner,
where lies a man apparently badly wounded, and
crying like a child. I had seen him brought in on
a stretcher, but in the confusion had not noticed
where he had been taken. Dick halted, as we
arrived at the bed, looked at me, as much as to
say, "There, isn't that a case requiring attention?"
and then, as though quite satisfied to resign him
into my hands, trotted quietly off.

I stood a moment to take an observation — to
make a sort of moral diagnosis before beginning
my attack — to find out whether the man needed
direct or indirect sympathy. Very often, to a
severely wounded man—not of a nervous temperament, but suffering intensely,—a kind word, showing that you appreciate and enter into that suffering, falls on the burning wound with a soothing,
cooling power, as beneficial, for the instant, as a
more visible application; on the wound, I say, for
the answer is, after a few minutes' conversation,

not, "Thank you, I feel better able to bear the
pain, now;" but, "Thank you, my arm doesn't
burn as much as it did — my limb isn't so painful
— my head feels cooler, now." But, on the other
hand, who that has suffered from unstrung nerves
does not know that what is most needed in such a
case, is to divert the mind from itself—to present
suddenly some other image powerful enough to
efface from it the impressions of its own wretched
self—to enable it to rouse itself and rise above the
weakness it is ashamed of, but has no power to
conquer? Any allusion to the suffering itself, in
such a case, only adds fuel to the flame.

I had time to draw my own conclusions, and soon
decided that Dick's protegé belonged to this latter
class. He did not notice my approach; I therefore
stood watching him for a little while. His arm
and hand, from which the bandage had partially
slipped, were terribly swollen; the wound was in
the wrist, (or rather, as I afterwards found, the
ball had entered the palm of his hand and had
come out at his wrist,) and appeared to be, as it
subsequently proved, a very severe one.

My boast that I could make a pretty good con-
jecture what State a man came from by looking at
him, did not avail me here. I was utterly at fault.
His fair, Saxon face, so far as I could judge of it
as he lay sobbing on his pillow, had something
feminine—almost childlike—in the innocence and

gentleness of its expression; and my first thought was one which has constantly recurred on closer acquaintance, "How utterly unfit for a soldier!" He wanted the quick, nervous energy of the New Englander, who, even when badly wounded, rarely fails to betray his origin; he had none of the rough off-hand dash of our Western brothers, and could never have had it, even in health; nor yet the stolidity of our Pennsylvania Germans. No! it was clear that I must wait till he chose to enlighten me as to his home. After a few minutes' study, I was convinced that his tears were not from the pain of his wound; there was no contraction of the brow, no tension of the muscles, no quivering of the frame; he seemed simply very weary, very languid, like a tired child, and I resolved to act accordingly.

"I have been so busy with our defenders, this afternoon," said I, "that I have had no time to come and thank you."

He started, raised his tear-stained face, and said, with a wondering air, "To thank me? For what?"

"For what?" said I; "haven't you been keeping the rebels away from us? Don't you know that if it hadn't been for you and many like you, we might at this moment have been flying from our homes, and General Lee and his men occupying our city? You don't seem to know how grateful we are to you—we feel as though we could never do enough for our brave Gettysburg men to return what they have done for us."

This seemed quite a novel idea, and the tears were stopped to muse upon it.

"We tried to do our duty, ma'am, I know that."

"I know it too, and I think I could make a pretty good guess what corps you belong to. Suppose I try. Wasn't it the Second Corps? You look to me like one of General Hancock's men; you know they were praised in the papers for their bravery. Am I right?"

The poor tired face brightened instantly. The random shot had hit the mark.

"Yes, Second Corps. Did you know by my cap?"

"Your cap? You don't wear your cap in bed, do you? I haven't seen your cap; I guessed by that wound—it must have been made where there was pretty hard fighting, and I knew the Second Corps had done their share of that."

But this was dangerous ground, as I felt the moment the allusion to his wound was made; the sympathy was too direct, and his eyes filled at once. Seeing my mistake, I plunged off rapidly on another tack.

"Did you notice my assistant orderly who came in with me just now? He had been over to see you before, for he came and told me you wanted me."

18

"I wanted you! No, ma'am; that's a mistake; no one's been near me since they bathed me, and gave me clean clothes—I know there hasn't, for I watched them running all about; but none came to me, and I want so much to have my arm dressed." And the ready tears once more began to flow.

"There is no mistake. I told you that my assistant orderly came to me in the ladies' room, and told me that you needed me. Think again—who has been here since you were brought in?"

"Not a single soul, ma'am,—indeed, not a thing, but a dog, standing looking in my face, and wagging his tail, as if he was pitying me."

"But a dog! Exactly; he's my assistant orderly; he came over to me, pulled my dress, and wouldn't rest till I came to see after you. I am surprised you speak so slightingly of poor Dick."

Here was at once a safe and fertile theme. I entered at large upon Dick's merits; his fondness for the men — his greater fondness, occasionally, for their dinners—his having made way with three lunches just prepared for men who were starting— (the result, probably, of having heard the old story that the surgeons eat what is intended for the men,) our finding him one day on our table with his head in a pitcher of lemonade, and how I had tried to explain to him that such was not the best way of proving his regard for his friends, the soldiers, but I feared without much effect — in short, I made a

long story out of nothing, till the wardmaster
arrived with his supper, saying that the doctor's
orders were that the new cases should all take
something to eat before he examined their wounds.
My friend had quite forgotten his own troubles in
listening to Dick's varied talents, and allowed me
to give him his supper very quietly, as I found he
was really too much exhausted even to raise his
uninjured arm to his mouth. I had the pleasure
of seeing him smile for goodbye, and having given
him rather more time than I could spare, hurried
away, with a promise of seeing him the next day
(Sunday), for they were too ill not to be watched.

But oh! for a little more daylight! It is getting
so dark, and yet I must stop and make acquaintance with each new face — or rather, I long to do
so, but it will not be possible. Look at those clear
blue eyes, over there — just what the French call
" les yeux de velours !"—I cannot surely pass them
without a word; they smile a welcome as I approach.
What a contrast their owner presents to poor Still-
well, my tearful friend, whom I have just left. A
sweet, bright face, clear complexion, curling light
hair, and something very winning in his open,
frank expression, which attracts you to him at
once. Before he opens his lips I am persuaded
that he possesses a cheerful spirit, ready to look
on the bright side of everything.

"You don't look as though you were suffering much; I hope you're not badly wounded."

What a beaming, beautiful smile, as he extends his hand to me at once!

"Oh! no; not badly, only hit in the shoulder; it's pretty painful, but I guess I'll be all right in a few days."

How little could I imagine, from his words, what I found out a few days later, that I was standing at that moment by one of the very worst wounds that had come in. The surgeon of the ward told me that he considered it a most critical case, and that, had the shot gone one half inch further, it must have been certainly fatal. It seemed that Dick and I between us, had discovered the two most severely wounded men in the whole hospital. For many weeks after that they were dangerously ill, requiring close and careful watching every hour, but rewarding us in the end with the hope of perfect recovery.

"I am glad to hear it," said I, in answer to his too sanguine view of his wound, "for you don't look as if you had seen much sickness, and maybe you wouldn't bear it very well."

"I've never been a day in bed in my life before this, and I hardly know what to make of it. I'm an Ohio boy, used to the country and living in the open air, and I couldn't stand being shut up here at all; it's as bad as the Libby prison."

Fancy my horror. Our hospital compared to the Libby prison!

"Oh! you mustn't say that; we try to do everything here to make the confinement as easy as possible to the men, and to help them to forget that it is a hospital. I'm sure you can't have been in the 'Libby' ever, have you?"

"Oh! no, indeed, never; but it seems just as bad to me to be fastened in here."

"Well, some day, soon, I will bring you in some of our men who have been there; let them talk to you and give you their experience, and then, when you know us better, I will ask you whether you still think the same. But now I must really say good-night. I will come to the 'prison,' to-morrow, to see how you all are."

"Thank you; you'll be very welcome; and maybe," added he, laughing, "it won't seem so like it when I get at home here;" and once more extending his hand, he said "good-night."

So ended the memorable week of July, 1863, which followed the glorious Gettysburg fight.

The tide of war has rolled back from our homes; the highly strung nerves are calmed; the dead sleep in the quiet graves which a people's love has provided for them on the field of their fame; the wounded, so lately massed in our midst, are scattered; some — too few, alas! — returned, cured, to their regiments; others (the saddest part of the

18 *

war) discharged from service, disabled and crippled for life; while for the remainder, listen to the words of that pale boy — as I raise his head to give him the needed stimulant, the notes of music fall on my ear.

"What is that, Henry?"

"What is that, do you ask, Miss ——? That is only some of our poor Gettysburg boys *going home;*" and I recognize the dead march, and I see the reversed arms, as the mournful train winds by.

Time has gone on; new faces, new forms, have filled the places of the old ones, and still our labors, our hopes, our Prayers, continue for our dear and bleeding country; still continues, also, our abiding faith and trust in the ultimate triumph of the right; and, leaving the event in Higher Hands, fearlessly we abide the issue.

THE END.

www.ingramcontent.com/pod-product-compliance
Lightning Source LLC
Chambersburg PA
CBHW030825270326
41928CB00007B/899